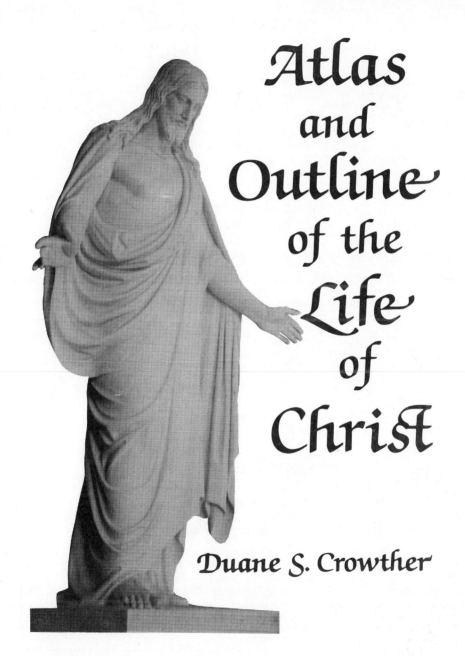

Atlas
and
Outline
of the
Life
of
Christ

Duane S. Crowther

International Standard Book Number
0-88290-207-5

Library of Congress Catalog Card Number
82-82414

Horizon Publishers Catalog and Order Number
1070

Printed and Distributed in the
United States of America

by

**Horizon
Publishers &
Distributors, Inc.**

———————

**50 South 500 West
P.O. Box 490
Bountiful, Utah 84010**

About the Cover: The world-famous statue of "The Christus" was sculpted by the Danish artist Thor Valdsen (1770-1844). The original stands in The Church of Our Lady cathedral in Copenhagen, Denmark, along with twelve other statues of Christ's apostles which he made. He devoted much of his life to the project, utilizing the years 1820-1842 for their creation.

PREFACE

The Purpose of This Book—a "Handy Study Guide"

This *Atlas and Outline of the Life of Christ* has been prepared to serve as a simple but detailed guide to studying the life and teachings of the Master. From the inception of the project, the challenge has been to keep it as short and unencumbered as possible, while still recording all the Savior's travels, sermons, parables, miracles, and other significant experiences detailed or alluded to in the four gospels. Its preparation has been a labor of love—love for the Savior, love for the scriptures, and love for the uplifting influence felt by those who study the life of their Redeemer and strive to pattern their life after his. It is my sincere desire that it may be a useful and inspirational tool to all who use it.

As more than one reader has observed, this small volume is "loaded" with useful information. It is far more comprehensive than any harmony of the gospels in print at the present time. But it is designed to be a "handy study guide," not a scholarly work of great profundity. To maintain its brevity, I have elected to omit references other than those found in the scriptures, and to refrain from making extensive commentaries (that was hard to do!), for there are many hundreds of interesting sidelights that cried out to be discussed. But to consider them would be to defeat the major objective of the book: to provide a brief, portable, easily utilized aid to understanding the order of events, the travels, and the teachings of our Lord.

Problems of Dating and Chronological Order

There are almost as many conflicting views concerning the dating and chronological order of the life of Jesus Christ as there are Biblical scholars. There is no unanimity as to his date of birth. The Biblical records do not tell us with precision the length of his life. Emminent theologians are divided in their views as to whether his ministry lasted one, two, or three years. Even the four gospels vary in their reporting of the order of events in our Savior's life.

As this outline was being prepared, it was debated whether to include dates, seasons, and chronological relationships. It was recognized that many such notes, at best, would be expressions of opinion rather than fact. It was recognized, also, that this brief outline format would allow scant room for documentation or commentary. Yet it was felt that the inclusion of these helps would be of value to the reader, and would aid him in making his own observations as he studied the life of the Master. While readily acknowledging the possibility of error in the areas of dating and chronological order within the book, I still felt that more dating information, rather than less, would be of greatest benefit to the reader.

This background is included for every chronological entry. Though it may seem somewhat repetitive to one who reads large portions of the outline, yet it was included on an every-item basis to accommodate those who will occasionally look up a brief passage without devoting time to an extensive reading of its context.

The general concensus of Biblical scholarship today seems to place the birth of Jesus Christ in the spring of 5 B.C., prior to the death of Herod the Great in 4 B.C. (Mt. 2:1, 13-15). Many scholars believe his ministry began at about the age of 30 (based primarily on the comment in Lk. 3:23), in the spring of 26 A.D. John indicates three Passovers took place during his ministry, so the most commonly advanced view is that Christ's ministry lasted three full years, with his crucifixion coinciding with the fourth Passover in April of 30 A.D. This general outline has formed the basis for the dating provided herein. It is acknowledged, of course, that various eminent scholars hold conflicting views, but this outline remains in the mainstream of Biblical scholarship, which places his life between 5 B.C. and 30 A.D., and is generally in agreement with the most accepted datings for Christ's life and ministry. It is assumed that the reader is somewhat aware of the calendar corrections which placed Jesus' birth several years "before Christ." Those changes and their implications concerning the year of his birth are not discussed herein.

Uncertainty of Routes Traveled

Another problem exists in the matter of the routes traveled by the Savior during his ministry. No one, of course, knows the exact routes he followed in most of his journeys. A map showing the main roads of his day has been provided, but the problems of readability and route uncertainty have made it necessary to show his travels more or less "as the crow flies," on subsequent maps, rather than attempting to faithfully adhere to the road system of his day.

But despite the limitations mentioned above, there is much in this brief outline that will be of value to those who use it to aid them in their study of the life of our Lord and Savior, Jesus Christ. May it prove a blessing in their life, as it has been for me as I prepared it. And may we always be found

In His Service,

Duane S. Crowther

CONTENTS

USE THIS EFFECTIVE FOUR-GOSPEL
BIBLE MARKING SYSTEM

The outline found in this book can serve as the basis for a simple but very efficient Bible marking system. Since it deals only with chronology, and utilizes only the page margins, it can be easily superimposed over other color codes and doctrinal identification systems. Here's how to set it up in your Bible:

1. **Write the number of each event in the margin beside the verse in which the event begins.** Do this in all four gospels. Example:

> *41* 14 But Jŏhn forbad him, saying, I have need to be baptized of thee, and comest thou to me?

2. **Underline the event number if it constitutes the "best" reference.** (In this outline, the most important reference is listed first for each event. Feel free to evaluate the verses from each gospel and substitute your personal choices when necessary.) Example:

> *16* 7 And she brought forth her firstborn son, and wrapped him in swaddling clothes, and laid him in a manger; because there was no room for them in the inn.

3. **Record the period name and/or number at the top of each page.** You may wish to add dates and other information also. Example:

Period 11 Christ's Resurrection and Ascension
Sun. Apr. 9, 30 A.D. to May 18, 30 A.D.

4. **Identify every major discourse, by writing the discourse number and complete reference by its beginning verse.** Example:

Discourse #2
Jn. 4:5-27

If you will utilize this system, or some adaptation of it, you'll know at a glance, on every page of the four gospels:

A. What period of Christ's life is being discussed.
B. In what verse every new event begins.
C. Which events are not following the normal reading order.
D. Where every major discourse begins and ends.
E. Whether you're reading the most detailed account of each event.

And you'll be completely keyed to this book, which will then serve as a master index to the four gospels. This system can be completely installed in your Bible in less than a day. Do it now, and enjoy it for a lifetime!

CHRIST'S NATIVITY AND PREPARATION

(From the Birth of John the Baptist to the Beginning of John's Ministry)

7 B.C. to 26 A.D.

Matthew 1-2   Luke 1-2   John 1:1-14

The Birth of John the Baptist
The Birth of Jesus the Christ
The Flight into Egypt
The Death of Herod the Great
The Division of Herod's Kingdom

1. The Preface of St. John (Jn 1:1-14).

2. The Preface of St. Luke (Lk.1:1-4).

3. **The genealogies of Christ's mortal parents (Mt. 1:1-17; Lk. 3:23-38).**

Note: **Royal and Personal Pedigrees**—As commentators analyze the differences in the genealogical lineages given by Matthew and Luke, some assert that Matthew presents the royal lineage of Joseph, showing the legal successors to the throne of David, while Luke presents the personal pedigree of Joseph through natural descent. Others believe that Matthew gives Joseph's personal lineage, while Luke gives Mary's.

4. **The birth of John the Baptist foretold to his father, Zacharias, by the angel Gabriel (Lk 1:5-22).** *Temple of Herod, Jerusalem; Oct., 7 B.C. (The course of Abia [Abijah] is believed to have officiated in the temple in April and October.)* ★ [1]

---

1. This outline is intended as a non-denominational study guide which focuses primarily on historical and geographical aspects of the life of Christ, rather than doctrinal issues. However, to aid in the study of doctrinal patterns, stars (★) have been placed by passages containing significant doctrinal items. Major discourses of the Savior have also been identified and numbered.

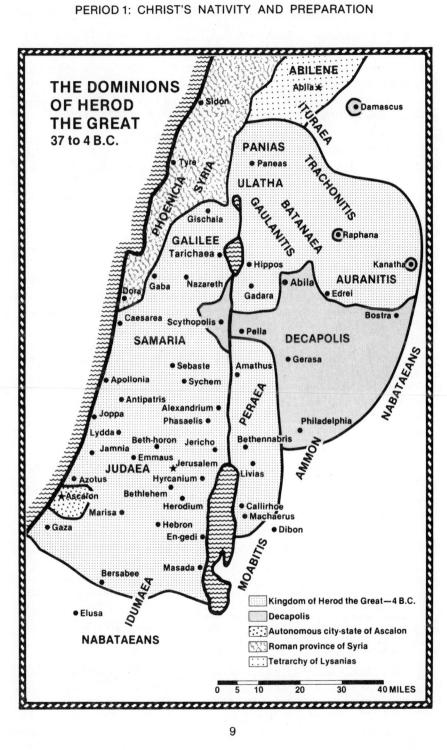

THE DOMINIONS OF HEROD THE GREAT
37 to 4 B.C.

ABILENE

Abila ✶

Sidon

Damascus

ITURAEA

PANIAS

Paneas

TRACHONITIS

Tyre

ULATHA

PHOENICIA

SYRIA

GAULANITIS

BATANAEA

Gischala

GALILEE

Raphana

Tarichaea

Kanatha

Hippos

AURANITIS

Nazareth

Dora   Gaba

Abila

Gadara

Edrei

Caesarea   Scythopolis

Bostra

Pella

DECAPOLIS

SAMARIA

Gerasa

Sebaste

Amathus

NABATAEANS

Apollonia

Sychem

Antipatris

PERAEA

Alexandrium

Joppa

Phasaelis

Philadelphia

Lydda

Beth-horon   Jericho

Bethennabris

Jamnia

AMMON

Emmaus

Jerusalem

JUDAEA

Livias

Azotus

Hyrcanium

Ascalon

Bethlehem

Marisa

Herodium

Callirhoe
Machaerus

Gaza

Hebron

Dibon

En-gedi

MOABITIS

Bersabee

Masada

IDUMAEA

Elusa

NABATAEANS

░ Kingdom of Herod the Great—4 B.C.
▓ Decapolis
░ Autonomous city-state of Ascalon
▧ Roman province of Syria
░ Tetrarchy of Lysanias

0   5   10   20   30   40 MILES

9

5. Zacharias departed to his own house (Lk. 1:23). *(Jewish tradition says he was a native of Hebron; some scholars have also suggested that his home was in Juttah, which is probably modern Yatta.) Jerusalem to Hebron(?); Nov., 7 B.C.*

6. Elizabeth conceived; five months of her pregnancy passed (Lk. 1:24-25). *Hebron(?); Fall, 7 B.C.—Spring, 6 B.C.*

7. The angel Gabriel foretold the birth of Jesus to Mary: "That holy thing which shall be born of thee shall be called the Son of God" **(Lk. 1:26-38).** *Nazareth; In the sixth month of Elizabeth's pregnancy; July(?), 6 B.C.* ★

8. Mary visited Elizabeth about three months: "My soul doth magnify the Lord" **(Lk. 1:39-56).** *Nazareth to Hebron(?); Summer(?), 6 B.C.* ★

Note: **The Magnificat**—Verses 46-55, great words of praise unto God, are often sung in church services. They are known as "The Magnificat."

9. Mary returned to Nazareth (Lk. 1:56). *Hebron(?) to Nazareth; shortly before, or just after, John's birth, Sept.(?), 6 B.C.*

10. The birth, circumcision, and naming of John the Baptist (Lk. 1:57-66). *Hebron(?); Sept. or Oct.(?), 6 B.C.*

11. The prophecy of Zacharias: "Thou, child, shalt be called the prophet of the Highest" **(Lk. 1:67-79).** *Hebron(?), at the circumcision of John the Baptist; Sept. or Oct.(?), 6 B.C.* ★

Note: **The Benedictus**—Verses 68-79 are sung in some churches, and are known as "The Benedictus."

12. An angel foretold the birth and mission of Jesus to Joseph: "Thou shalt call his name JESUS: for he shall save his people from their sins" **(Mt. 1:18-23).** *Nazareth; Sept. or Oct.(?), 6 B.C.* ★

13. The marriage and relationship of Joseph and Mary (Mt. 1:24-25).

14. The tax decree of Caesar Augustus (Lk. 2:1-2). *Rome; Fall, 6 B.C. or Winter, 5 B.C.*

Note: **Caesar Augustus**—Gaius Octavius was born in Rome September 23, 63 B.C., and became influential through his great uncle, Julius Caesar, who adopted him and made him his heir. When Julius Caesar was murdered in 44 B.C., Gaius grew in influence, and finally became the emperor after defeating his rival, Antony, at the battle of Actium, September 2, 31 B.C. The beginning of the Roman empire is reckoned from that date, and he was the first Roman emperor. The Roman senate gave him the title "Augustus." He reigned until 14 A.D.

Note: **Cyrenius**—Historians now believe that Cyrenius [Quirinius] was not the Roman civil governor of Syria until 6 A.D. He may, however, have been there as a "legatus Caesaris" to conduct the census under the direction of the governor, who was either Sentius Saturninus, 9-6 B.C., or Quinctilius Varus, 6-4 B.C.

15. Joseph and Mary journeyed from Nazareth to Bethlehem (Lk. 2:3-5). *March - April(?), 5 B.C.*

Note: **The Season of Christ's Birth**—The actual day of the Lord's birth is unknown. The traditional December 25th date was first observed in Constantine's time,

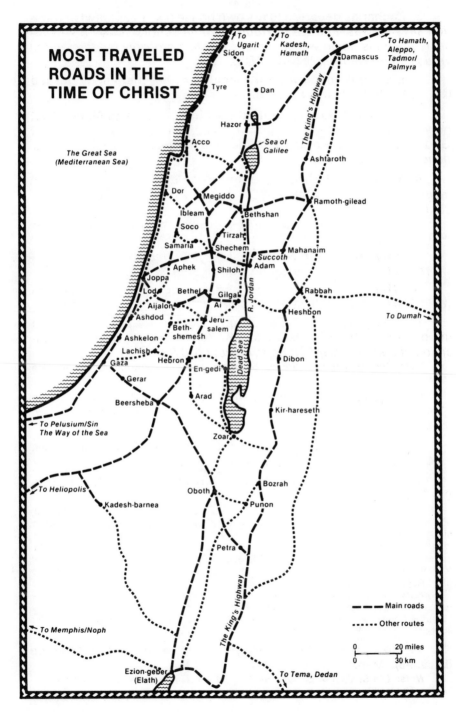

MOST TRAVELED ROADS IN THE TIME OF CHRIST

THE JEWISH YEAR

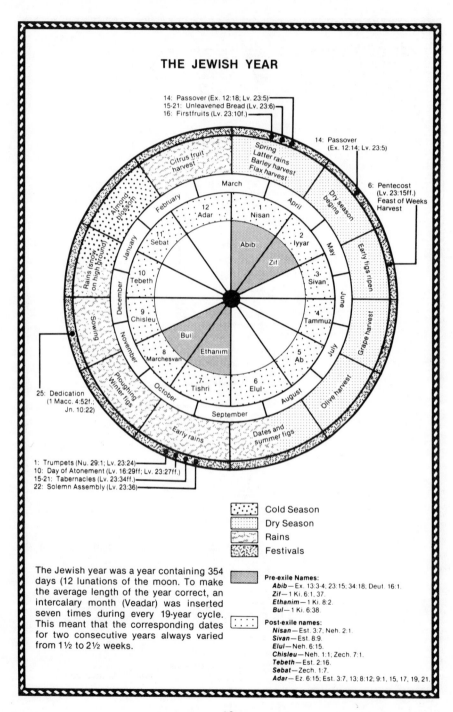

14: Passover (Ex. 12:18; Lv. 23:5)
15-21: Unleavened Bread (Lv. 23:6)
16: Firstfruits (Lv. 23:10f.)

14: Passover (Ex. 12:14; Lv. 23:5)

6: Pentecost (Lv. 23:15ff.) Feast of Weeks Harvest

Spring
Latter rains
Barley harvest
Flax harvest

Dry season begins

Early figs ripen

Grape harvest

Olive harvest

Dates and summer figs

Citrus fruit harvest

Almond blossom

Rains (snow on high ground)

Sowing

Ploughing
Winter figs

Early rains

25: Dedication (1 Macc. 4:52f., Jn. 10:22)

1: Trumpets (Nu. 29:1; Lv. 23:24)
10: Day of Atonement (Lv. 16:29ff; Lv. 23:27ff.)
15-21: Tabernacles (Lv. 23:34ff.)
22: Solemn Assembly (Lv. 23:36)

March — 12 Adar — 1 Nisan — Abib
11 Sebat — April — 2 Iyyar — Zif
February — May — 3 Sivan
January — 10 Tebeth — June — 4 Tammuz
December — 9 Chisleu — Bul — Ethanim — July — 5 Ab
November — 8 Marchesvan — August
October — 7 Tishri — 6 Elul
September

Cold Season

Dry Season

Rains

Festivals

Pre-exile Names:
Abib—Ex. 13:3-4; 23:15; 34:18; Deut. 16:1.
Zif—1 Ki. 6:1, 37.
Ethanim—1 Ki. 8:2.
Bul—1 Ki. 6:38.

Post-exile names:
Nisan—Est. 3:7; Neh. 2:1.
Sivan—Est. 8:9.
Elul—Neh. 6:15.
Chisleu—Neh. 1:1; Zech. 7:1.
Tebeth—Est. 2:16.
Sebat—Zech. 1:7.
Adar—Ez. 6:15; Est. 3:7, 13; 8:12; 9:1, 15, 17, 19, 21.

The Jewish year was a year containing 354 days (12 lunations of the moon. To make the average length of the year correct, an intercalary month (Veadar) was inserted seven times during every 19-year cycle. This meant that the corresponding dates for two consecutive years always varied from 1½ to 2½ weeks.

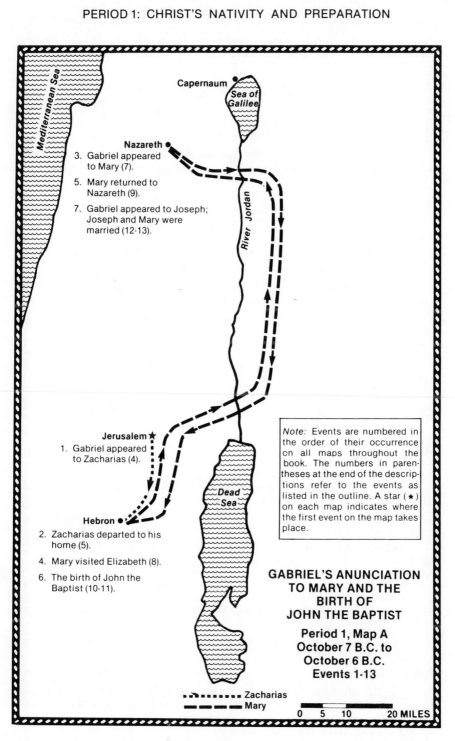

Mediterranean Sea

Capernaum

Sea of Galilee

Nazareth ●
3. Gabriel appeared to Mary (7).

5. Mary returned to Nazareth (9).

7. Gabriel appeared to Joseph; Joseph and Mary were married (12-13).

River Jordan

Jerusalem ★
1. Gabriel appeared to Zacharias (4).

Dead Sea

Note: Events are numbered in the order of their occurrence on all maps throughout the book. The numbers in parentheses at the end of the descriptions refer to the events as listed in the outline. A star (★) on each map indicates where the first event on the map takes place.

Hebron ●
2. Zacharias departed to his home (5).

4. Mary visited Elizabeth (8).

6. The birth of John the Baptist (10-11).

GABRIEL'S ANUNCIATION TO MARY AND THE BIRTH OF JOHN THE BAPTIST

**Period 1, Map A
October 7 B.C. to
October 6 B.C.
Events 1-13**

▪▪▪▪▪▪▪▪▪ Zacharias
▬ ▬ ▬ ▬ Mary

0   5   10   20 MILES

325 A.D., and was officially set by the Roman church in the 4th century. (The Greek Orthodox Church celebrates January 6th, the Armenian Church January 19th.) It is believed that the birth of Christ did not take place in the winter, since Palestinian shepherds usually kept their flocks under cover from the November rains until the Passover (March or April) and the "latter rains" of those months. April is lambing season, when shepherds are caring for newborn animals in the fields around-the-clock. Many scholars assert that Jesus, the "Lamb of God" (Jn. 1:29), was born in April, at the season when other Passover lambs were born.

16. The birth of Jesus the Christ (Lk. 2:6-7; Mt. 1:25; Jn. 1:14). *Bethlehem; April(?), 5 B.C. If Christ was born in 5 B.C. (a leap year), it would have been in the year of the Romans 749.*

Note: Traditional Site of Christ's Birth—The Church of the Nativity, built over the 11′ × 38′ cave where it is believed Jesus was born, is the oldest church in Christendom. It was originally constructed by Constantine about 330 A.D., after his mother, Helena, determined the site.

17. Angels appeared to Bethlehem shepherds (Lk. 2:8-15). *Near Bethlehem; April(?), 5 B.C.* ★

18. The shepherds visited the baby Jesus (Lk. 2:15-20). *Bethlehem, the night of Jesus' birth; April(?), 5 B.C.*

Note: Temple Flocks—Many of the flocks at Bethlehem were raised to be used as temple sacrifices. The shepherds who cared for them held a higher social position than other shepherds, who were usually social outcasts.

19. The circumcision of Jesus (Lk. 2:21). *Bethlehem; eight days after his birth, April, 5 B.C.*

20. Jesus was presented in the Jerusalem temple (Lk. 2:22-24). *Temple of Herod, Jerusalem; forty days after his birth, May, 5 B.C.*

21. Simeon came to see Jesus in the temple: "Mine eyes have seen thy salvation" **(Lk. 2:25-35).** *Temple of Herod, Jerusalem; May, 5 B.C.* ★

22. The witness of Anna the prophetess (Lk. 2:36-38). *Temple of Herod, Jerusalem; May, 5 B.C.*

23. Wise men from the east journeyed to Judea and inquired of Herod the king (Mt. 2:1-8). *Jerusalem; 5 or 4 B.C.*

Note: Herod the Great—Herod was the third ruler in an Idumean family which had been converted to the Jewish faith, and which established a semi-independent kingdom under the protection of Rome. Herod succeeded his father, Antipater. He married Mariamne to ally himself with the family of the Maccabees. He built Caesarea, the Temple of Herod at Jerusalem, several fortresses and other buildings. His was a cruel reign; he even had his wife and three of his sons murdered. He ruled Judea from 37 to 4 B.C.

24. The wise men were led by a star to the house where Jesus was (Mt. 2:9-12). *Bethlehem(?), Jerusalem(?), or Nazareth (see Lk. 2:39); 5 or 4 B.C. (Time had passed—the family was in a house.)*

25. An angel warned Joseph to flee to Egypt with Jesus and Mary (Mt. 2:13). *Bethlehem(?), Jerusalem(?), or Nazareth(?); shortly after the departure of the wise men, 5 or 4 B.C.*

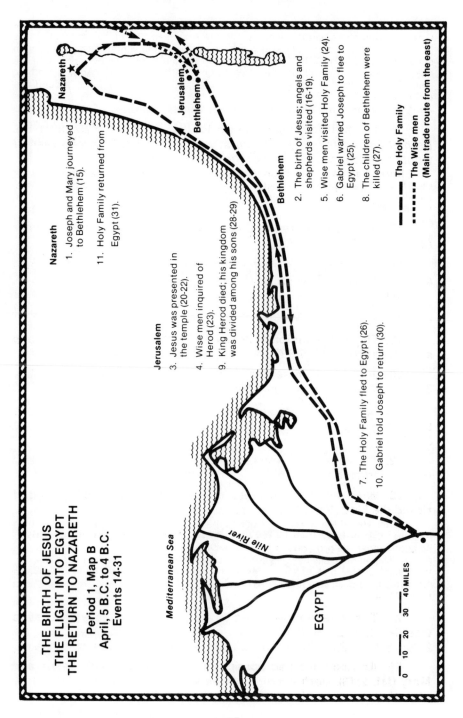

THE BIRTH OF JESUS
THE FLIGHT INTO EGYPT
THE RETURN TO NAZARETH

Period 1, Map B
April, 5 B.C. to 4 B.C.
Events 14-31

Nazareth

1. Joseph and Mary journeyed to Bethlehem (15).

11. Holy Family returned from Egypt (31).

Jerusalem

3. Jesus was presented in the temple (20-22).

4. Wise men inquired of Herod (23).

9. King Herod died; his kingdom was divided among his sons (28-29).

Bethlehem

2. The birth of Jesus; angels and shepherds visited (16-19).

5. Wise men visited Holy Family (24).

6. Gabriel warned Joseph to flee to Egypt (25).

8. The children of Bethlehem were killed (27).

7. The Holy Family fled to Egypt (26).

10. Gabriel told Joseph to return (30).

The Holy Family

The Wise men
(Main trade route from the east)

Mediterranean Sea

Nile River

EGYPT

0   10   20   30   40 MILES

26. Joseph, Jesus and Mary fled to Egypt (Mt. 2:14-15). *Palestine to Egypt; until the death of Herod, 5 or 4 B.C.*
Note: Tradition Concerning Where Jesus Lived in Egypt—Visitors to Cairo, Egypt, often visit Saint Sergius's Coptic Church (Abu Serga). Under the altar is a cave, which tradition asserts is where Joseph, Mary, and Jesus lived until their return to Palestine.

27. Herod ordered the slaughter of the children of Bethlehem (Mt. 2:16-18). *Bethlehem; 5 or 4 B.C. (Some commentators point out that Bethlehem was so small that this may only have involved 20 or 30 children, rather than thousands.)*

28. The death of Herod the Great (Mt. 2:15, 19). *Jerusalem; It is believed his death occurred about the 13th of Adar (March), 4 B.C.*

29. Herod's kingdom was divided between three of his sons. *Jerusalem; 4 B.C.*
Note: The Tetrarchies of Archelaus, Antipas, and Philip: When Herod died, Augustus Caesar divided Herod's kingdom among his sons. Archelaus (Mt. 2:22) received Judea, Idumea and Samaria. Herod Antipas (Mt. 14:1; Lk. 9:7; Mk. 6:14—known as king Herod and Herod the tetrarch) ruled Galilee and Peraea. Philip received Ituraea (the northeast districts of Palestine). *Tetrarchy* means "one-fourth of a kingdom."

30. An angel instructed Joseph to take Mary and Jesus back to the land of Israel (Mt. 2:19-20). *Cairo(?), Egypt; 4 B.C.*

31. Joseph, Mary, and Jesus journeyed to Nazareth and dwelt there (Mt. 2:21-23). [Compare Lk. 2:39] *Cairo(?), Egypt, to Nazareth; 4 B.C.*

32. Jesus grew in spirit, wisdom, and the grace of God (Lk. 2:40). *Nazareth; 4 B.C. - 8 A.D.*

33. Joseph and Mary attended the Passover in Jerusalem every year (Lk. 2:41). *Nazareth to Jerusalem to Nazareth; each spring.*

34. Jesus went to the Passover in Jerusalem when he was twelve, and spent time in the temple: "Wist ye not that I must be about my Father's business?" **(Lk. 2:42-49).** *Nazareth to Jerusalem; April, 8 A.D.*

35. Jesus returned to Nazareth and was subject to his parents (Lk. 2:51). *Jerusalem to Nazareth; 8 - 26 A.D.*

36. Jesus increased in wisdom and stature, and in favor with God and man (Lk. 2:52). *Nazareth; 8 - 26 A.D.*

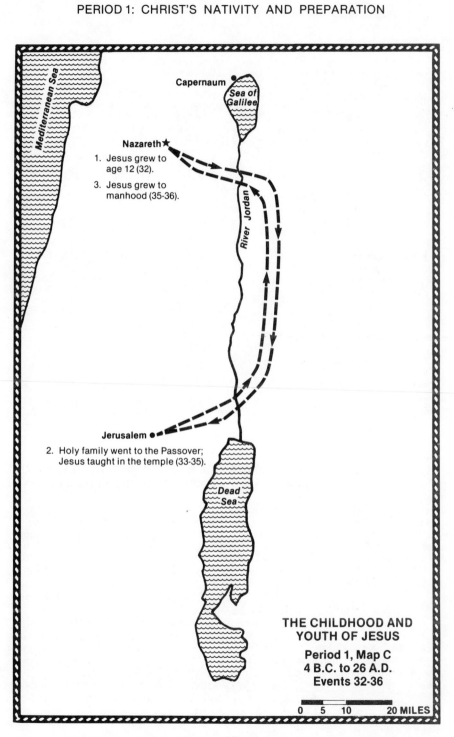

Mediterranean Sea

Capernaum

Sea of Galilee

Nazareth ★

1. Jesus grew to age 12 (32).

3. Jesus grew to manhood (35-36).

River Jordan

Jerusalem ●

2. Holy family went to the Passover; Jesus taught in the temple (33-35).

Dead Sea

THE CHILDHOOD AND YOUTH OF JESUS

**Period 1, Map C
4 B.C. to 26 A.D.
Events 32-36**

0   5   10   20 MILES

Period 2

CHRIST'S PRELIMINARY MINISTRY

(From the Beginning of John's Ministry to the First Passover of Christ's Ministry)

Summer, 26 A.D. to March-April, 27 A.D.

Matthew 3-4:11 Mark 1:1-13 Luke 3-4:13 John 1:15-2:12

The Baptism of Jesus
His Temptation in the Wilderness
John the Baptist's Testimony of Jesus
The Calling of John, Peter, Andrew,
   Philip and Nathanael
The Marriage Feast in Cana

---

37. The political world at the time of Jesus' ministry (Lk. 3:1-2).

A. Tiberius Caesar ruled as emperor of the Roman empire (ruled 14-37 A.D.)

Note: **Tiberius**—Tiberius Julius Caesar Augustus (born 42 B.C.), became the second Roman emperor when Augustus, his step-father, died. He reigned throughout all of Christ's ministry, and died March 16, 37 A.D. He was an able general and a competent emperor, though he put many of his supposed rivals to death.

Note: **Fifteenth Year**—Tiberius served as co-emperor of Rome with Augustus for over a year before Augustus died. This dating probably reaches back to the beginning of that co-ruler interregnum.

B. Pontius Pilate was Procurator (governor) of the Roman province of Judea (26-36 A.D.).

Note: **Pontius Pilate**—Pontius Pilatus succeeded Valerius Gratus as procurator of Judea in 26 A.D. He was disliked by the Jews because of his anti-Jewish acts, and they several times went over his head to Caesar, who compelled Pilate to yield to the Jewish demands. He stayed at Caesarea and ruled from there, but would come to Jerusalem and make the Antonia Fortress his headquarters during the Jewish feasts. When Tiberius died, Pilate was not reappointed to his post in Judea.

C. Herod Antipas was Tetrarch of Galilee, a semi-independent kingdom (4 B.C. - 39 A.D.).

18

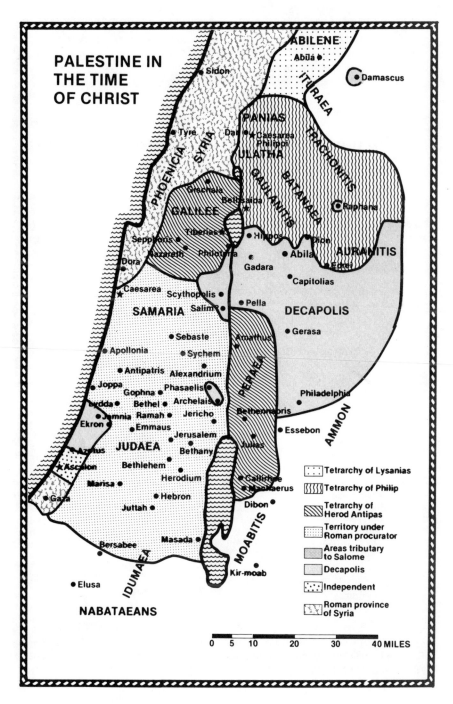

PALESTINE IN
THE TIME
OF CHRIST

ABILENE

Abila

Damascus

Sidon

ITURAEA

Tyre · Dan · Caesarea
Philippi

PANIAS

PHOENICIA

SYRIA

ULATHA

TRACHONITIS

Gischala

BATANAEA

Bethsaida

GAULANITIS

GALILEE

Raphana

Tiberias

Sepphoris

Hippos · Dion

Nazareth · Philoteria

AURANITIS

Dora

Gadara · Abila

Edrei

Caesarea

Capitolias

Scythopolis

Pella

SAMARIA · Salim?

DECAPOLIS

Sebaste

Amathus

Gerasa

Apollonia · Sychem

PERAEA

Antipatris · Alexandrium

Joppa · Gophna · Phasaelis

Lydda · Bethel · Archelais

Jamnia · Ramah · Jericho

Philadelphia

Ekron

Bethennabris

Emmaus

Esrebon

Jerusalem

AMMON

JUDAEA · Bethany

Julias

Azotus · Bethlehem

Ascalon · Herodium

Callirhoe

Marisa · Machaerus

Hebron · Dibon

Gaza · Juttah

Masada

MOABITIS

Bersabee

IDUMAEA

Kir-moab

Elusa

NABATAEANS

	Tetrarchy of Lysanias
	Tetrarchy of Philip
	Tetrarchy of Herod Antipas
	Territory under Roman procurator
	Areas tributary to Salome
	Decapolis
	Independent
	Roman province of Syria

0   5   10   20   30   40 MILES

19

D. Philip (Herod Antipas' brother) was Tetrarch of Ituraea, a semi-independent kingdom (4 B.C. - 33 A.D.).
E. Lysanias (identity unknown) was Tetrarch of Abilene.
F. Annas was a former Jewish high priest who still held considerable influence.

Note: **Annas**—Annas (abbreviated form of Hananiah) was appointed high priest (the highest Jewish religious office) in 7 A.D. by the Roman legate Quirinius but was deposed in 15 A.D. by Valerius Gratus. As was Jewish custom, he kept his title "high priest" after being removed from office. Five of his sons also became Jewish high priests.

G. Caiaphas was the Jewish high priest.

Note: **Caiaphas**—Joseph Caiaphas, son-in-law of Annas, served as high priest from 18-36 A.D. He belonged to the Sadducee party.

38. John the Baptist preached and baptized near the Jordan River: "Repent ye: for the kingdom of heaven is at hand" **(Mt. 3:1-6; Lk. 3:3-6; Jn. 1:15-18(?); Mk. 1:1-6).** *Wilderness of Judea near the Jordan River (a 10-mile wide tract west of the Dead Sea, including the mouth of the Jordan River; chief towns: Engedi and Tekoa); Summer(?), 26 A.D.* ★

39. John's confrontation with the Sadducees and Pharisees; he prophesied of Jesus: "He that cometh after me . . . shall baptize you with the Holy Ghost, and with fire" **(Mt. 3:7-12; Lk. 3:7-18; Mk. 1:7-8).** [Compare Jn. 1:19-28] *Near the Jordan River; Fall(?), 26 A.D.* ★

Note: **Sadducees and Pharisees**—These were the two main religious sects in the time of Christ. The *Sadducees* accepted only the law and rejected oral tradition; they denied resurrection, immortality, angels, and the spirit world (Mk. 12:18; Lk. 20:27; Acts 23:8). They were a relatively small group, but were the elite, and held and controlled the office of high priest. They supported the Maccabeans, but looked mostly to Rome for support. They were denounced by both John the Baptist and Jesus. The *Pharisees* were the most influential party, and were the strictest of the Jewish sects (the "separatists," who supposedly separated themselves from evil). They wore distinguishing clothing so they could be easily recognized. They believed in Jewish tradition, as well as law, and pledged to obey both in every detail. They were constantly concerned about ceremonial purity. They were hostile to foreign rule. They looked for a Messiah to come, but saw that coming from a very nationalistic viewpoint. They believed in predestination, immortality, the spirit world, revelation, that the spirits of the wicked were imprisoned forever under the earth, and that the virtuous would rise again and even migrate to other bodies. They believed they were the only interpreters of God's word. Jesus condemned their long public prayers, frequent fasts, arrogance, hypocrisy, impenitence, and their emphasis on salvation by works. They were closely allied with the scribes and lawyers.

40. Jesus came from Nazareth to the Jordan River (Mt. 3:13; Mk. 1:9). *Nazareth to the River Jordan; Fall(?), 26 A.D.*

41. Jesus was baptized by John; the Holy Ghost descended in the form of a dove, and the Father spoke from the heavens: "This is my beloved Son, in whom I am well pleased" **(Mt. 3:14-17; Lk. 3:21-22; Mk. 1:9-11)** [Compare Jn. 1:32-34] *Unidentified location on the Jordan River (not necessarily Bethabara, traditionally just north of the Dead Sea; Fall(?), 26 A.D.* ★

42. Jesus became 30 years old (Lk. 3:23).

Note: Dating Problems—This verse says "Jesus himself began to be about thirty years of age." The verse is so ambiguous that it is unclear whether he was baptized before his birthday or after he reached 30; and this is the only verse which provides any substantial scriptural clue to his age during his ministry.

43. Jesus returned from the Jordan River, then was led by the Spirit into the wilderness where he was tempted by Satan, and angels ministered to him: "Jesus said . . . Thou shalt not tempt the Lord thy God" (Mt. 4:1-11; Lk. 4:1-13; Mk. 1:12-13). *Jordan River to Nazareth (Lk. 4:1), to an unknown wilderness area, back to Nazareth(?). During the temptation Satan took him to the high roof of the temple (where Roman soldiers often were posted to overlook the crowds during feast days), then to a high mountain (tradition asserts that this was Mt. Quarantana (near Jericho, where the Greek Monastery of the Forty Days now stands). Fall(?), 26 A.D.* ★

44. John answered the priests from Jerusalem: "I am not the Christ. . . . I am the voice of one crying in the wilderness, Make straight the way of the Lord" (Jn. 1:19-28). *Bethabara beyond (east of) Jordan, where John was baptizing; Fall(?), 26 A.D.* ★

Note: The Uncertain Chronological Relationship of Jn. 1:18-2:12—One of the most perplexing questions when preparing a harmony of the gospels is "where do these verses fit?" Is Jn. 1:19-28 the same as Mt. 3:7-12 (#39, above), or is it a later event? Is Jn. 1:29-34 another account of Christ's baptism (#41, above), or is it a separate testimony born by John? John shows events happening on five consecutive days (see Jn. 1:29, 35, 43; 2:1), in which Jesus moves from Bethabara (location unknown) across Galilee into Cana. All these events, when seen in this chronological relationship, appear to be different than those reported in the other three gospels. And his brief visit to Capernaum (Jn. 2:12), just before the first passover (Jn. 2:13) appears to be a separate visit, prior to his early Galilean ministry (see Period 4). These verses are placed in several different chronological relationships by various scholars, and their order is, at best, uncertain.

45. Jesus visited John the Baptist, and John testified to his followers of Christ: "I saw, and bare record that this is the Son of God" (Jn. 1:29-34). *Bethabara (location unknown, but near Galilee—within a day's journey of Cana); next day after John the Baptist answered the priests from Jerusalem, Fall(?), 26 A.D.* ★

46. Jesus met three of the disciples of John the Baptist: John, Andrew and Simon Peter: "We have found the Messias" (Jn. 1:35-42). [Compare Mt. 4:18-21; Mk. 1:16-20] *Unknown location near Galilee; next day after John the Baptist testified Jesus was the Son of God, the tenth hour (4 p.m.), Fall(?), 26 A.D.* ★

47. Jesus started into Galilee and met Philip and Nathaniel: "Rabbi, thou art the Son of God; thou art the king of Israel" (Jn. 1:43-51). *Enroute to Galilee, unknown location; next day following the call of John, Andrew and Peter, Fall(?), 26 A.D.* ★

Note: Nathanael—This is probably another name for the apostle Bartholomew (see Mt. 10:3).

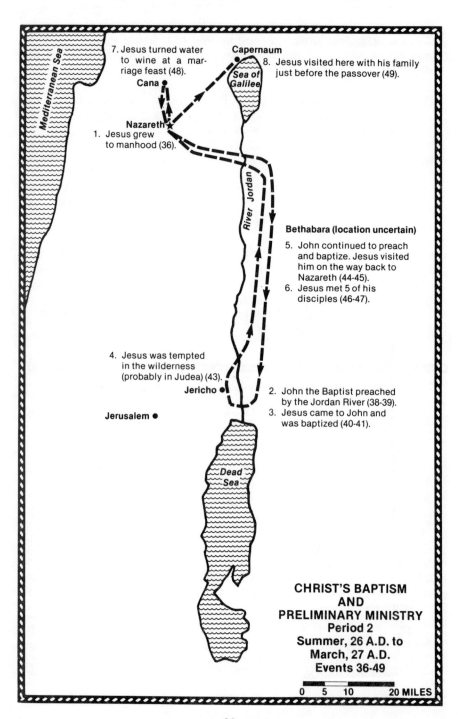

7. Jesus turned water to wine at a marriage feast (48).

Capernaum

8. Jesus visited here with his family just before the passover (49).

Sea of Galilee

Cana

Nazareth
1. Jesus grew to manhood (36).

River Jordan

Mediterranean Sea

Bethabara (location uncertain)

5. John continued to preach and baptize. Jesus visited him on the way back to Nazareth (44-45).
6. Jesus met 5 of his disciples (46-47).

4. Jesus was tempted in the wilderness (probably in Judea) (43).

Jericho

Jerusalem

2. John the Baptist preached by the Jordan River (38-39).
3. Jesus came to John and was baptized (40-41).

Dead Sea

**CHRIST'S BAPTISM
AND
PRELIMINARY MINISTRY
Period 2
Summer, 26 A.D. to
March, 27 A.D.
Events 36-49**

0   5   10   20 MILES

48. Jesus turned water into wine at a marriage feast in Cana, which he attended with his mother and his disciples (Jn. 2:1-11). *Cana; next day following the call of Philip and Nathanael, Fall(?), 26 A.D.*

49. Jesus stayed in Capernaum "not many days" with his mother, brothers, and disciples (Jn. 2:12). *Nazareth(?) (after several months?) to Capernaum; just before Passover time, March, 27 A.D.*

Note: **Jesus' Family**—Since Jesus' father, Joseph, is mentioned in the accounts of Christ's ministry, it is assumed that he passed away sometime after Jesus was twelve but before he was thirty. Jesus had at least four brothers (James, Joses [Joseph], Simon, and Judas), plus two or more sisters (see Mt. 13:55-56).

Note: **Jesus' Early Disciples**—It appears that his early disciples numbered at least six: Peter, Andrew, James, John, Philip and Nathanael, and that they were with him during his visit to Cana, and later to Capernaum. This may have been a period of intense training for them.

Chronological Observation Concerning Period 2: It is obvious that there are two "clusters" of events which transpired during this preparatory period: Christ's baptism and temptation (reported in the synoptic gospels), and the series of day-by-day events recorded by John. Of the approximately nine-month period, with its indefinite beginning, less than two months are reported. But it concludes with the first calendar-related event of Christ's ministry: preparation for the Passover feast to be celebrated at Jerusalem (Jn. 2:13).

ISRAEL'S CLIMATE

Israel has a general climate and temperature range similar to Florida. January and February are the coldest months, and August is the warmest. The Mediterranean Sea exerts strong climatic influence. The rainy season is comparatively short, and there are three to four completely rainless summer months. The following are the monthly mean temperatures in Tel Aviv and in Jerusalem:

	Tel Aviv		Jerusalem	
	Centigrade	*Fahrenheit*	*Centigrade*	*Fahrenheit*
January	13.7	56.7	9.7	49.5
February	14.3	57.7	11.6	52.9
March	17.2	63.0	13.8	56.8
April	19.1	66.4	17.7	63.9
May	21.3	70.3	21.3	71.0
June	22.5	72.5	23.7	74.7
July	24.1	75.4	24.4	75.9
August	24.8	76.6	25.0	77.0
September	23.6	74.5	23.9	75.0
October	22.3	72.1	21.8	71.2
November	18.7	65.7	17.2	63.0
December	15.2	59.4	12.3	54.1

Period 3

CHRIST'S EARLY JUDEAN MINISTRY

(From the First Passover of Christ's Ministry to His Return to Galilee)

April, 27 A.D. to December, 27 A.D.

Matthew 4:12   Mark 1:14   Luke 4:14   John 2:13-4:44
(Imprisonment of John the Baptist: Mt. 14:3-5; Mk. 6:17-20; Lk. 3:19-20)

The First Passover of Christ's Ministry
The Cleansing of the Temple
Jesus' Teachings to Nicodemus
Jesus Taught and Gained Many Converts in Judea
Herod Imprisoned John the Baptist
Jesus Taught the Samaritan Woman

50. Jesus went up to Jerusalem to celebrate the Passover (Jn. 2:13). *Capernaum(?) to Jerusalem; Passover dates: April 11-18, 27 A.D.*

51. Jesus drove the merchants and their animals out of the temple: "Make not my Father's house an house of merchandise" (Jn. 2:14-17). [Compare Mt. 21:12-13; Mk. 11:15-17; Lk. 19:45-46] *Temple of Herod, Jerusalem; mid-April, 27 A.D.*

52. Jesus answered the Jews who asked for a sign: "Destroy this temple, and in three days I will raise it up" (Jn. 2:18-22). [Compare Mt. 26:61] *Temple of Herod, Jerusalem; same day, mid-April, 27 A.D.* ★

53. Jesus did many miracles, and many believed in his name during the Passover (Jn. 2:23-25). *Jerusalem; April 11-18, 27 A.D.*

54. Jesus taught Nicodemus, a member of the Jewish Sanhedrin: "Ye must be born again, . . . God so loved the world, that he gave his only begotten Son" (Jn 3:1-21). *The home of John(?) in Jerusalem; at night, during the Passover, mid-April, 27 A.D.* [★ — Major Discourse #1]

Note: **The Sanhedrin**—Nicodemus, a Pharisee, was a member of the Sanhedrin (Jn. 7:50). This was the Jewish senate and highest court in both ecclesiastical and civil disputes. It consisted of 71 members, including the high priest who presided over it, and drew its members from the Jewish aristocracy: the chief priests, the scribes, and the elders. Most of its members were either Pharisees or Sadducees, and the Pharisees were in the majority. The Sanhedrin had great power, its own police officers, and its decisions were regarded as binding throughout the Jewish world, though the Roman authority still superceded it.

55. Jesus and his disciples came into the land of Judea; he tarried with them and baptized (Jn. 3:22). *Judea; Summer-Fall, 27 A.D.*

56. John the Baptist also baptized farther north (Jn. 3:23-24). *Aenon (means "springs"), near to Salim (close to Seythopolis?); John was not yet in prison, Summer, 27 A.D.*

57. John testified to his disciples about Christ: "He must increase, but I must decrease" (Jn. 3:25-36). *Aenon; Summer, 27 A.D.* ★

58. Herod Antipas, the Tetrarch, imprisoned John the Baptist (Mk. 6:17-20; Lk. 3:19-20; Mt. 14:3-5). *John was imprisoned in the Fortress of Machaerus, east of the Dead Sea; Summer(?), 27 A.D.*

Note: **Herod Antipas**—Called "the Tetrarch" (Mt. 14:1; Lk. 3:19; 9:7; Acts 13:1), he was a son of Herod the king (Mt. 2:3). He was made Tetrarch (means "ruler over a fourth of the kingdom") over Judea and Perea when his father died in 4 B.C. He built Tiberias, on the Sea of Galilee, to be his capitol. He unlawfully took Herodias, wife of his half-brother Philip, as his wife. Jesus called him a "fox" (Lk. 13:32). In his rivalry with Herod Agrippa I, he asked the Roman emperor Caligula to grant him the title of king. This aroused Roman suspicion, and the emperor eventually banished him to Gaul in 39 A.D.

59. Jesus made and baptized more disciples than John the Baptist (Jn. 4:1-2). *Judea; Summer-Fall, 27 A.D.*

60. Jesus left Judea, and journeyed towards Galilee through Samaria (Jn. 4:3; Mt. 4:12; Mk. 1:14). *Judea to Samaria; Dec., 27 A.D.*

Note: **Avoiding Conflict with the Pharisees and with Herod Antipas**—Judea was the center of strength of the Pharisees; Jesus left the area to avoid direct confrontation with them. He knew that Herod had imprisoned John, and to avoid the same fate, he did not follow the main road (The King's Highway) which passed through Peraea (the seat of Herod's power), but instead went through Samaria.

61. Jesus taught the Samaritan woman at Jacob's well: "Whosoever drinketh of the water that I shall give him shall never thirst" (Jn. 4:5-27). *Judea to Jacob's well, near Sychar, Samaria; the sixth hour (noon), Dec., 27 A.D.* **[★ —Major Discourse #2]**

Note: **Samaritans**—The Samaritans were of foreign origin, for their forefathers had been brought to the land by the Assyrians seven centuries previous (see 2 Ki. 17:24-34). Though they had partially accepted Judaism, they were ostracised by the Jewish inhabitants of Palestine, and were treated with contempt.

62. The Samaritan woman brought others from Sychar to meet the Christ (Jn. 4:28-30). Sychar, Samaria; afternoon of the same day, Dec., 27 A.D.

63. Jesus taught his disciples at Jacob's well: "My meat is to do the will of him that sent me, and to finish his work" (Jn. 4:31-38).

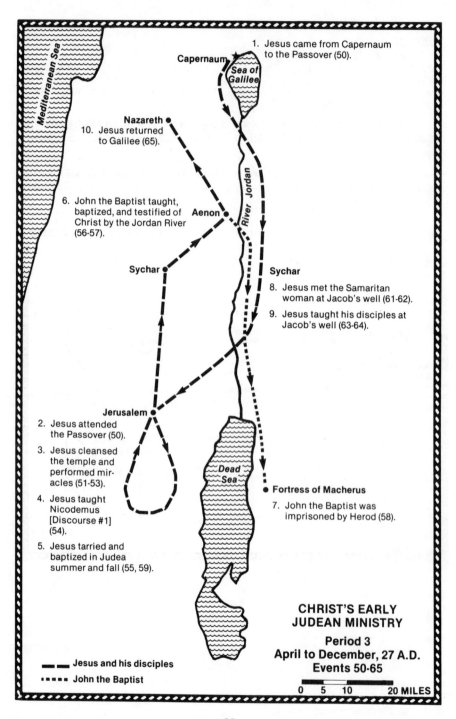

1. Jesus came from Capernaum to the Passover (50).

10. Jesus returned to Galilee (65).

6. John the Baptist taught, baptized, and testified of Christ by the Jordan River (56-57).

Sychar

8. Jesus met the Samaritan woman at Jacob's well (61-62).

9. Jesus taught his disciples at Jacob's well (63-64).

2. Jesus attended the Passover (50).

3. Jesus cleansed the temple and performed miracles (51-53).

4. Jesus taught Nicodemus [Discourse #1] (54).

5. Jesus tarried and baptized in Judea summer and fall (55, 59).

Fortress of Macherus

7. John the Baptist was imprisoned by Herod (58).

Mediterranean Sea

Capernaum

Sea of Galilee

Nazareth

Aenon

River Jordan

Sychar

Jerusalem

Dead Sea

CHRIST'S EARLY JUDEAN MINISTRY

Period 3
April to December, 27 A.D.
Events 50-65

— — Jesus and his disciples

••••• John the Baptist

0   5   10   20 MILES

Jacob's well, near Sychar, Samaria; Dec. (four months before harvest), 27 A.D. ★

Note: Harvest—The agricultural year began the last half of October, when the early rains softened the ground baked by the summer heat. Harvest time began earliest in the semi-tropical Jordan Valley and latest in the uplands of Galilee. The average harvest lasted seven weeks (Lev. 23:15; Deut. 16:9), from the middle of April to the beginning of June.

64. Jesus and his disciples stayed two days at Sychar with the Samaritans, and many believed in him (Jn. 4:39-42). *Sychar, Samaria, Dec., 27 A.D.* ★

65. Jesus and his disciples came into Galilee, the Galileans received him (Jn. 4:43-45). *Samaria to Galilee (Nazareth?); his Galilean disciples probably went to their homes; Dec., 27 A.D.* ★

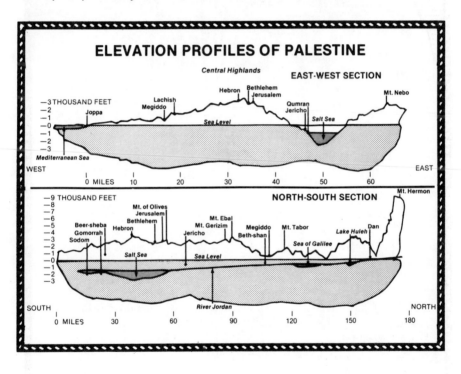

27

Period 4

CHRIST'S EARLY GALILEAN MINISTRY

(From Christ's Return to Cana Through the Calling of the Twelve, to the Second Passover)

December, 27 A.D. to April, 28 A.D.

Matthew 4:13-8:5   Mark 1:15-3:19
Matthew 8:14-17
Matthew 9:2-17   Luke 4:14-6:49
Matthew 10:1-42
Matthew 12:1-21   John 5:1-47

Jesus Healed the Nobleman's Son
Jesus was Rejected at Nazareth, and
    Made Capernaum His Home
The Sermon on the Mount
Jesus Healed a Man Lowered Through the Roof
The Feast at Matthew's Home
Conflict with the Pharisees
    Concerning the Sabbath
Jesus Called and Ordained Twelve Apostles
The Sermon on the Plain
Jesus Attended a Feast in Jerusalem, and
    Healed a Man at the Pool of Bethesda

66. **Jesus went again to Cana (Jn. 4:46).** *Nazareth(?) to Cana; Winter, 27-28 A.D.*

67. **Jesus told a nobleman from Cana, whose son was near death in Capernaum, that his son would live. The son's fever left him that same hour (Jn. 4:46-54).** *Nobleman: Cana to Capernaum; Winter, 28 A.D.*

68. Jesus taught in the synagogues of Galilee (Lk. 4:14-15). *Galilee; Winter, 27-28 A.D.*

Note: Synagogues—Synagogues began during the Babylonian captivity. By Christ's time there were synagogues in every Jewish town and village large enough to have an adult congregation of ten men. They were directed by local self-governing bodies called "elders," who were also the rulers of the local community in both religious and civil affairs. A "ruler of the synagogue" maintained order and decided who would conduct the service. An "attendant" had charge of the building, and served during the week as schoolmaster.

69. Jesus preached in the synagogue at Nazareth: "No prophet is accepted in his own country" **(Lk. 4:16-28).** [Compare Mt. 13:54-58; Mk. 6:1-6] *Nazareth synagogue; on the sabbath, Winter, 28 A.D.* *[★ —Major Discourse #3]*

70. The people of Nazareth rejected Jesus, thrust him out of the city, and attempted to take his life (Lk. 4:29-30). *Nazareth, at edge of city's hill; the same day, Winter, 28 A.D.*

71. Jesus left Nazareth, and came and dwelt in Capernaum (Mt. 4:13-16). *Nazareth to Capernaum; Winter, 28 A.D.*

72. Jesus began to preach, saying "Repent: for the kingdom of heaven is at hand" **(Mt. 4:17; Mk. 1:15).** *Capernaum; Winter, 28 A.D.*

73. Jesus, walking by the Sea of Galilee, called Simon Peter and his brother, Andrew, back to his ministry: "Follow me, and I will make you fishers of men" **(Mk. 1:16-18; Mt. 4:18-20).** [Compare Lk. 5:1-11] *Sea of Galilee, near Capernaum; Winter, 28 A.D.*

74. Jesus called James and John to leave their ship and follow him (Mk. 1:19-20; Mt. 4:21-22). [Compare Lk. 5:1-11] *Sea of Galilee, near Capernaum; the same day, Winter, 28 A.D.*

75. Jesus and his disciples went into Capernaum, and Jesus taught with power and authority in the synagogue on the sabbath day (Mk. 1:21-22; Lk. 4:31-32). *Capernaum synagogue; the next Sabbath(s), Winter, 28 A.D.*

76. Jesus cast unclean spirits out of a man in the Capernaum synagogue, and his fame spread round about (Mk. 1:23-28; Lk. 4:33-37). *Capernaum synagogue; on a Sabbath day, Winter, 28 A.D.*

77. Jesus healed the fever of Simon's mother-in-law (Mk. 1:29-31; Lk. 4:38-39; Mt. 8:14-15). *Simon's house, Capernaum; the same day, Winter, 28 A.D.*

78. Jesus healed many of the inhabitants of Capernaum, and cast out many devils (Mk. 1:32-34; Lk. 4:40-41; Mt. 8:16-17). *Simon's house, Capernaum; the same day at sunset, Winter 28 A.D.*

79. Jesus arose before sunup to pray in the desert. When Simon and the other disciples found him, he told them he had to preach to other cities also (Mk. 1:35-38; Lk. 4:42-43). *Desert near Capernaum; early the next morning, Winter, 28 A.D.*

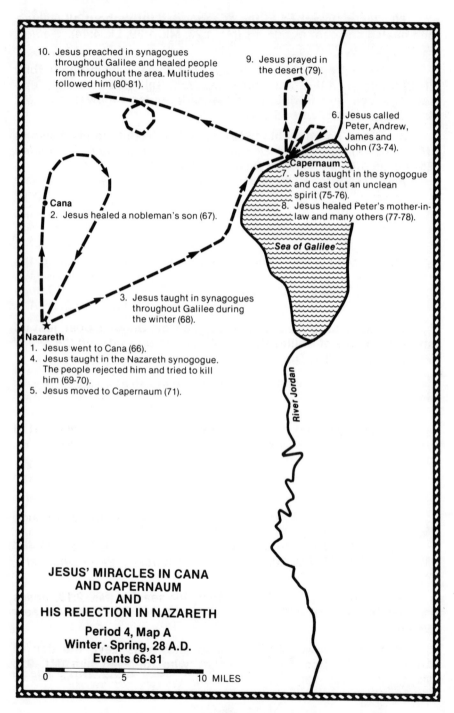

10. Jesus preached in synagogues throughout Galilee and healed people from throughout the area. Multitudes followed him (80-81).

9. Jesus prayed in the desert (79).

6. Jesus called Peter, Andrew, James and John (73-74).

Capernaum

7. Jesus taught in the synogogue and cast out an unclean spirit (75-76).

8. Jesus healed Peter's mother-in-law and many others (77-78).

Cana
2. Jesus healed a nobleman's son (67).

Sea of Galilee

3. Jesus taught in synagogues throughout Galilee during the winter (68).

Nazareth
1. Jesus went to Cana (66).
4. Jesus taught in the Nazareth synogogue. The people rejected him and tried to kill him (69-70).
5. Jesus moved to Capernaum (71).

River Jordan

**JESUS' MIRACLES IN CANA
AND CAPERNAUM
AND
HIS REJECTION IN NAZARETH**

**Period 4, Map A
Winter - Spring, 28 A.D.
Events 66-81**

0   5   10 MILES

30

80. Jesus preached in the synagogues throughout all Galilee, and healed and cast out devils (Mt. 4:23; Mk. 1:39; Lk. 4:44). *Galilee; Winter-Spring, 28 A.D.*

81. Jesus' fame spread throughout Syria, who brought their sick for him to heal. Great multitudes from Galilee, Decapolis, Jerusalem, Judea, and from beyond [east of] Jordan followed him (Mt. 4:24-25). *Galilee, Winter-Spring, 28 A.D.*

82. Jesus delivered his "Sermon on the Mount" to his disciples (Mt. 5:1-7:29). [Compare Lk. 6:20-49] *On a mountain in Galilee; Spring, 28 A.D.* *[★ —Major Discourse #4]*
Note: The Sermon on the Mount and the Sermon on the Plain—Scholars are divided as to whether or not the sermon recorded in Mt. 5-7 is the same as Luke recorded in Lk. 6, after the calling of the Twelve. Some hold that it is the same discourse delivered on two different occasions to different audiences; others hold that it is two different versions of the same event and feel that Luke's account is most accurate, though Matthew's has more detail.

83. Jesus healed a leper, who widely published his healing; the crowds grew so great he could no longer preach in the cities (Mk. 1:40-45; Mt. 8:1-4; Lk. 5:12-15). *In a city near the mountain in Galilee where the Sermon on the Mount was given; same day, Spring, 28 A.D.*

84. Jesus taught a crowd of people from Simon's boat, just off shore in the Sea of Galilee (Lk. 5:1-3). *On Simon's boat on the Sea of Galilee; Spring, 28 A.D.*
Note: Gennesaret—The lake of Gennesaret was another name for the Sea of Galilee. Gennesaret was the fertile plain on the west shore, about one mile wide and two and one-half miles long, towards the north end. This shoreline area is about 500 feet below the level of the Mediterranean Sea.

85. Jesus helped his disciples catch a miraculous draught of fishes (Lk. 5:4-11). *On Simon's boat on the Sea of Galilee; same day, Spring, 28 A.D.*

86. Jesus withdrew into the wilderness and prayed (Lk. 5:16). *Galilee; Spring, 28 A.D.*

87. Jesus healed a man with the palsy who was lowered through the roof of the house: "But that ye may know that the Son of man hath power on earth to forgive sins . . . , Arise, and take up thy bed" **(Mk. 2:1-12; Lk. 5:17-26; Mt. 9:2-8).** *Jesus' house(?), Peter's house(?), Capernaum; Spring, 28 A.D.*

88. Jesus taught the multitude by the seaside (Mk. 2:13). *Jesus left the house, and went to the shore of the Sea of Galilee near Capernaum; same day, Spring, 28 A.D.*

89. Jesus called Matthew (also known as Levi, the son of Alphaeus), a customs tax collector), who followed him (Mt. 9:9; Mk. 2:14; Lk. 5:27-28). *Custom station, on the shore of the Sea of Galilee, Capernaum; same day, Spring, 28 A.D.*

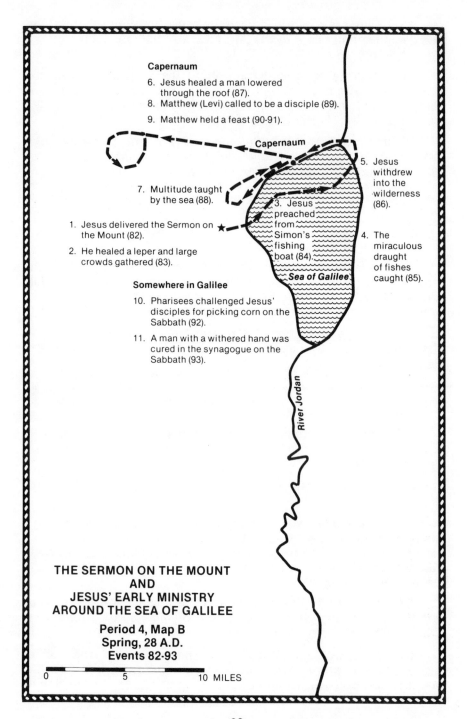

Capernaum

6. Jesus healed a man lowered through the roof (87).
8. Matthew (Levi) called to be a disciple (89).
9. Matthew held a feast (90-91).

Capernaum

5. Jesus withdrew into the wilderness (86).

7. Multitude taught by the sea (88).

1. Jesus delivered the Sermon on the Mount (82).

2. He healed a leper and large crowds gathered (83).

3. Jesus preached from Simon's fishing boat (84).

4. The miraculous draught of fishes caught (85).

Sea of Galilee

Somewhere in Galilee

10. Pharisees challenged Jesus' disciples for picking corn on the Sabbath (92).

11. A man with a withered hand was cured in the synagogue on the Sabbath (93).

River Jordan

**THE SERMON ON THE MOUNT
AND
JESUS' EARLY MINISTRY
AROUND THE SEA OF GALILEE**

**Period 4, Map B
Spring, 28 A.D.
Events 82-93**

0   5   10 MILES

90. Levi held a feast at which Jesus answered the murmerings of the scribes and Pharisees: "I came not to call the righteous, but sinners to repentance" **(Lk. 5:29-32; Mt. 9:10-13; Mk. 2:15-17).** *Levi's (Matthew's) home, Capernaum; Spring, 28 A.D.* ★

91. Jesus answered the disciples of John about fasting: "Can the children of the bridechamber mourn when the bridegroom is with them?" *Parable:* new cloth on an old garment. *Parable:* new wine into old bottles. **(Mt. 9:14-17; Mk. 2:18-22; Lk. 5:33-39).** *Levi's (Matthew's) home, Capernaum; during the feast, same day, Spring, 28 A.D.* ★

92. Jesus and his disciples plucked ears of corn on the Sabbath day; Jesus told the Pharisees: "The sabbath was made for man, and not man for the sabbath" **(Mk. 2:23-28; Lk. 6:1-5; Mt. 12:1-8).** *Galilee; Spring, 28 A.D.* ★
Note: Conflict with the Pharisees—This event records the beginning of Christ's active conflict with the Pharisees. Controversy about how to observe the Sabbath became a major factor in the hostility they increasingly held for Christ.

93. Jesus healed the withered hand of a man in the synagogue: "Is it lawful to do good on the sabbath days, or to do evil? to save life, or to kill?" **(Mk. 3:1-5; Lk. 6:6-10; Mt. 12:9-13).** *Unknown synagogue in Galilee; on another Sabbath, Spring, 28 A.D.*

94. The Pharisees met with the Herodians, plotting how to destroy Jesus (Mk. 3:6; Mt. 12:14; Lk. 6:11). *Unknown location; Spring, 28 A.D.*
Note: Herodians—Members of this Jewish political party were supporters of the Herod dynasty. They also supported the Romans, apparently hoping for their national kingdom to be restored through one of Herod's sons.

95. Jesus and his disciples withdrew to the sea. Great multitudes followed him there, and Jesus healed many (Mk. 3:7-8; Mt. 12:15-21) [Compare Mt. 4:24-25] *Sea of Galilee; Spring, 28 A.D.*

96. Jesus spoke to the multitude from aboard a boat; unclean spirits recognized him to be the Son of God (Mk. 3:9-12). *Sea of Galilee; Spring, 28 A.D.*

97. Jesus went into a mountain, and continued all night in prayer (Lk. 6:12). *Mountain in Galilee; Spring, 28 A.D.*

98. Jesus called his disciples to the mountain and ordained twelve of them to be apostles (Lk. 6:13-16; Mk. 3:13-19) *Mountain in Galilee; the next day, Spring, 28 A.D.*

99. Jesus delivered his "Sermon on the Plain" to his disciples and to a great multitude (Lk. 6:17-49) *On a plain near the mountain where he ordained the Twelve, and near Capernaum; the same day(?), Spring, 28 A.D.* **[★ —Major Discourse #5]**

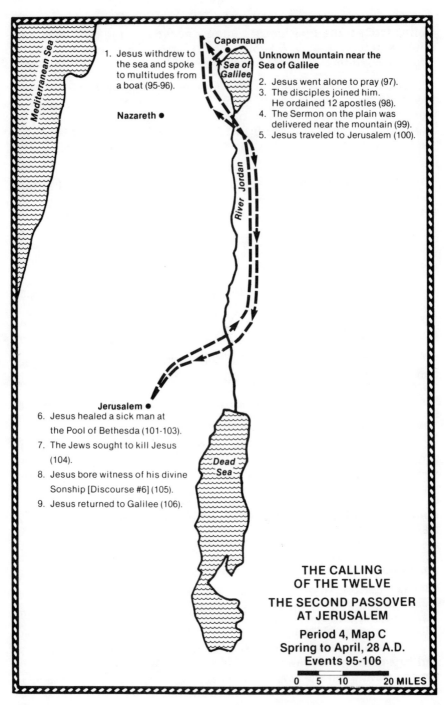

1. Jesus withdrew to the sea and spoke to multitudes from a boat (95-96).

Nazareth ●

Capernaum

Sea of Galilee

Unknown Mountain near the Sea of Galilee

2. Jesus went alone to pray (97).
3. The disciples joined him. He ordained 12 apostles (98).
4. The Sermon on the plain was delivered near the mountain (99).
5. Jesus traveled to Jerusalem (100).

River Jordan

Jerusalem ●

6. Jesus healed a sick man at the Pool of Bethesda (101-103).
7. The Jews sought to kill Jesus (104).
8. Jesus bore witness of his divine Sonship [Discourse #6] (105).
9. Jesus returned to Galilee (106).

Dead Sea

THE CALLING OF THE TWELVE

THE SECOND PASSOVER AT JERUSALEM

Period 4, Map C
Spring to April, 28 A.D.
Events 95-106

0 5 10 20 MILES

100. Jesus attended a feast in Jerusalem (the second Passover?) (Jn. 5:1) *Capernaum to Jerusalem; at the feast of Purim(?), March, or the Passover, April, 28 A.D.*

Note: **Passover or Purim**—The Passover feast commemorated the sparing of the Israelites when the firstborn of the Egyptians were slain (see Ex. 12:21-27). It was celebrated for seven days in the month of Abib [April], (Deut. 16:1-8), beginning on the 14th day (Lev. 23:5-14), and was combined with the feast of unleavened bread.

Some commentators believe the unnamed feast of John 5:1 was the feast of *Purim,* rather than the Passover. Purim, celebrated March 14 and 15 (Adar), commemorated the deliverance of the Jews from Haman, who plotted the extermination of the Jews throughout the Persian empire in 473 B.C. (see the book of Esther).

101. Jesus cured an impotent man by the pool of Bethesda: "Rise, take up thy bed, and walk" **(Jn. 5:2-9).** *The pool Bethesda, by the sheep market, in Jerusalem; on the Sabbath, Passover(?), April, 28 A.D.*

102. The jews rebuked the man Jesus healed for carrying his bed on the Sabbath day (Jn. 5:10-13). *Near the pool Bethesda; the same day, April, 28 A.D.*

103. Jesus found the man he had healed in the temple: "Sin no more, lest a worse thing come upon thee" **(Jn. 5:14).** *The Temple of Herod, Jerusalem; the same day, April, 28 A.D.* ★

104. The man Jesus healed told the Jews that it was Jesus who had made him whole; the Jews therefore persecuted Jesus and sought to slay him (Jn. 5:15-16). *Location unknown, Jerusalem; Passover(?), April, 28 A.D.*

105. Jesus bore witness of his divine Sonship to the Jews who persecuted him: "He that honoureth not the Son honoureth not the Father which hath sent him" **(Jn. 5:17-47).** *Location unknown, Jerusalem; Passover(?), April, 28 A.D. [★ —Major Discourse #6]*

106. Jesus returned to Galilee. [No scriptural reference.] *Jerusalem to Galilee; April, 28 A.D.*

Chronological Observations Concerning Period 4: The length of this period, and also the seasons involved, are based on the commonly made assumption that the feast attended by Jesus in Jerusalem (Jn. 5:1-47) is actually the second Passover, rather than another feast. This assumption is by no means certain, and various commentators (particularly those who do not believe the Savior's ministry extended for three years) disagree with it. John's record skips almost a full year between 5:1-47 and 6:4, which makes the establishment of the proper chronology for chapter 5 even more difficult.

Problems also exist when comparing the order of events as given in the synoptic gospels. Mark and Luke are generally in agreement during this period, while Matthew sometimes presents the same events in different time relationships.

THE TWELVE APOSTLES OF JESUS CHRIST

Simon Peter *(rock)*—Simon was the son of Jonah and the brother of Andrew. He was born in Bethsaida, but lived during Christ's ministry in a house in Capernaum with his wife and mother-in-law. He was a well-to-do fisherman in partnership with his father Jonah, Zebedee, Andrew, James and John. With James and John, he was in the inner circle of disciples closest to Jesus. He was the leader of the Church after Jesus' ascension, and wrote the two epistles of Peter. Tradition states that he was crucified upside down in Rome.

Andrew *(Manly)*—Andrew was the son of Jonah and Joanna and Simon's brother. He was a disciple of John the Baptist, and was probably the first to be called as Jesus' apostle. Tradition states that he was crucified in Achaia, tied to an X-shaped cross.

James *(James the Great. His name is the English form of Jacob)*—He was an older son of Zebedee and Salome, and probably a first cousin of Jesus (Salome was Mary's sister?). Jesus called James and John "Boanerges" (sons of thunder). James was the second disciple of the inner circle, and is believed to be the father of the apostle Jude. He was the second apostle to be killed, and was beheaded by Herod Agrippa (Acts 12:2).

John—He was the son of Zebedee and Salome, and therefore a brother of James, an uncle of Jude, and a first cousin of Jesus. He was called "the beloved," and was the third member of the inner circle. He was a fisherman, and a disciple of John the Baptist. He owned a home in Jerusalem. He wrote the gospel of John, the three epistles of John, and the book of Revelation. Jesus gave him the responsibility from the cross of caring for his mother. John preached in Ephesus, was exiled to Patmos, and was last heard of in Ephesus about 100 A.D. (See Mt. 27:3-5.)

Philip *(lover of horses)*—Philip was from Bethsaida and was a close friend of John and Andrew. He was a liberal Jew, and must have had some Greek influence in his life (his name is Greek and he served as a liason between Jesus and the Greeks). Tradition says he was crucified in Phrygia.

Bartholomew—Also known as **Nathanael** *(God has given)*—He was a son of Tolmai, from Cana, and of the tribe of Naphtali. He was usually named with Philip, and was called "an Israelite without guile" by Jesus. According to tradition, he was flayed, beheaded, or crucified in India or Armenia.

Thomas—Also called **Didymus** *(twin)*—He was a fisherman from Bethsaida, and a boyhood friend of John. Tradition states that he was killed by a lance in India or Persia.

Matthew—Also known as **Levi** *(gift of God)*—He was the son of Alphaeus and a brother of James the lesser, from Capernaum, and probably of the tribe of Levi. He was educated a Publican and tax collector in Capernaum, and was wealthy. He wrote the gospel of Matthew. Tradition asserts that he was killed by fire, sword or spear in Ethiopia.

James—A brother of Matthew, he was the son of Alphaeus and Mary (she is also identified as the wife of Cleophaus, another form of Alphaeus). He was from Capernaum, and of the tribe of Levi. His mother was probably a first cousin of Mary, the mother of Jesus. He may have been a Zealot. He was known as James the lesser, probably because he was younger or smaller than James the son of Zebedee. He is not James the brother of Jesus, who wrote the epistle of James and was leader of the Church in Jerusalem. Tradition confuses his death with that of Jesus' brother—one or both of them were thrown off the temple wall and then beaten to death by the Jews.

Lebbaeus *(hearty)*—Also known as **Thaddaeus** *(dear one)* and **Jude** (a derivitive of "Judah").—He was called the brother of James (Lk. 6:16). Tradition says he was the son of James the greater, thus being the grandson of Zebedee and the nephew of John, and first cousin once removed of Jesus. He was a fisherman, and of the tribe of Judah. He should not be confused with the brother of Jesus (Mt. 13:55). Tradition says he was crucified at Edessa or Persia.

Simon—Also called **Zelotes**—He was a fisherman from Cana, and probably was a member of the Zealots, a nationalistic sect that sought the overthrow of both the Jewish and Roman jurisdictions (this was the direct opposite of Matthew's views as a Publican). According to tradition, he preached in Britain and was crucified either in Britain or Persia.

Judas Iscariot—From Kerioth, Judas was the son of Simon, and of the tribe of Judah. He was the only disciple who was not from Galilee. He was the treasurer of the Twelve. He betrayed Jesus, and hung himself before Christ died (Mt. 27:3-5).

Period 5

CHRIST'S GREAT GALILEAN MINISTRY

(From After the Second Passover to the Time of the Third Passover)

April, 28 A.D. to April, 29 A.D.

Jesus Preached Throughout Galilee
Jesus Healed the Centurion's Servant
Jesus Raised the Son of the Widow of Nain
Jesus Spoke of John the Baptist
Jesus Ate with Simon the Pharisee
Jesus Gave His Burial as a Sign
The Day of Parables
Jesus Cast Out Demons at Gergesa
Jesus Raised the Daughter of Jairus
Jesus Sent Forth the Twelve to Preach
Herod Slew John the Baptist
Jesus Fed the 5,000
Jesus Walked on the Water
Jesus Gave His Sermon on the Bread of Life
Jesus Rebuked the Pharisees About
    Their Traditions

107. Jesus went to Capernaum (Lk. 7:1; Mt. 8:5). *Capernaum; the same day as the Sermon on the Plain was given(?), Spring A.D. 28.*

108. Jesus healed a Roman centurion's servant: "I have not found so great faith, no, not in Israel" **(Mt. 8:5-13; Lk. 7:2-10).** *Capernaum; the same day, Spring, 28 A.D.* ★

Note: **Roman Army Organization**—In the Roman army, a "Centurion" was a legionary officer who commanded a "century" composed of 50 to 100 infantrymen. He was roughly equivalent to a modern captain (though in social status was more like a non-commissioned officer). A "century" was a hundredth part of a legion, though in New Testament times Roman legions had only about 6,000 infantrymen, together with complements of other arms. A legion's infantry was divided into ten cohorts of 600 men, commanded by a "tribune." During Christ's time, the Roman army had 25 legions, four of which were stationed in Syria. Soldiers from local areas were used to supplement the Roman forces.

109. Jesus went to a city called Nain with his disciples and many people (Lk. 7:11). *Capernaum to Nain; the next day, Spring, 28 A.D.*

110. Jesus raised a widow's son from the dead. (Lk. 7:12-17). *Nain; the next day, Spring, 28 A.D.*

111. The disciples of John the Baptist told him of the miracles performed by Christ (Lk. 7:18). *Fortress of Machaerus, east of the Dead Sea; Summer, 28 A.D.*

112. John the Baptist sent two messengers to inquire of Jesus. They saw Jesus heal the sick. His instruction to the messengers was: "Tell John . . . the blind see, the lame walk, . . . the dead are raised, to the poor the gospel is preached" **(Lk. 7:19-23; Mt. 11:2-6).** *Unidentified location, Galilee; Summer, 28 A.D.*

113. Jesus spoke to the multitude about John the Baptist after the messengers departed: "There is not a greater prophet then John the Baptist" **(Mt. 11:7-15; Lk. 7:24-28).** *Unidentified location, Galilee; the same day, Summer, 28 A.D. [★ —Major Discourse #7, Mt. 11:7-30]*

114. When they heard Jesus' words, those baptized by John the Baptist justified God, but the Pharisees and lawyers rejected the counsel of God (Lk. 7:29-30). *Unidentified location, Galilee; the same day, Summer, 28 A.D.*

115. Jesus replied to the criticism of the Pharisees: "The Son of man is come eating and drinking; and ye say, Behold a gluttonous man, and a winebibber" **(Lk. 7:31-35; Mt. 11:16-19).** *Unidentified location, Galilee; the same day, Summer, 28 A.D.*

116. Jesus upbraided the cities wherein most of his mighty works were done (Chorazin, Bethsaida and Capernaum), because they did not repent (Mt. 11:20-24). *Unidentified location, Galilee; the same day, Summer, 28 A.D.*

117. Jesus prayed to his Father: "I thank thee . . . because thou hast hid these things from the wise and prudent, and hast revealed them unto babes" **(Mt. 11:25-27).** *Unidentified location, Galilee; the same day, Summer, 28 A.D.* ★

118. Jesus invited mankind to take his yoke upon them: "Come unto me, all ye that labor and are heavy laden, and I will give you rest" **(Mt. 11:28-30).** *Unidentified location, Galilee; the same day, Summer, 28 A.D.*

119. Jesus went to eat in the home of Simon, one of the Pharisees (Lk. 7:36). *Unidentified location, Galilee; Fall, 28 A.D.*

120. A woman of the city, a sinner, washed Jesus' feet with her tears and anointed them with ointment. Simon questioned Jesus' power of discernment in his mind (Lk. 7:37-39). [Compare Mt. 26:6-13; Jn. 12:2-8] *The home of Simon, the Pharisee, unidentified location, Galilee; Fall, 28 A.D.*

121. Jesus rebuked Simon the Pharisee and commended the sinful woman: "Her sins, which are many, are forgiven, for she loved much." *Parable:* The two debtors **(Lk. 7:40-50).** *The home of Simon the Pharisee, unidentified location, Galilee; during dinner, same day, Fall, 28 A.D.* ★

122. Jesus and the Twelve, accompanied by certain women, went throughout every city, showing the glad tidings of the kingdom of God (Lk. 8:1-3). *Throughout Galilee; Fall, 28 A.D.*

123. Jesus healed a blind and dumb man possessed with a devil (Mt. 12:22-23). *A house near the sea (Mt. 13:1), Capernaum(?); Fall, 28 A.D.*

124. Scribes and Pharisees from Jerusalem said that Jesus cast out devils by the power of the devil. Jesus replied, "If a kingdom be divided against itself, that kingdom cannot stand" **(Mt. 12:24-37; Mk. 3:22-30).** *Capernaum(?); the same day, Fall, 28 A.D.* **[★ —Major Discourse #8, Mt. 12:25-45]**

125. The scribes and Pharisees asked Jesus for a sign; Jesus answered, "The Son of man [shall] be three days and three nights in the heart of the earth" **(Mt. 12:38-45).** *Capernaum(?); the same day, Fall, 28 A.D.* ★

126. Jesus' mother and brothers came to see him: "My mother and my brethren are these which hear the word of God, and do it" **(Lk. 8:19-21; Mt. 12:46-50; Mk. 3:31-35).** *Capernaum(?); the same day, Fall, 28 A.D.*

127. Jesus began to teach again from a boat by the shore of the Sea of Galilee. Great multitudes gathered (Mt. 13:1-3; Mk. 4:1-2, Lk. 8:4). *Sea of Galilee; the same day, Fall, 28 A.D.*

128. Jesus told the parable of the sower to the multitude gathered by the sea (Mt. 13:3-9; Mk. 4:3-9; Lk. 8:5-8). *On a boat, Sea of Galilee; the same day, Fall, 28 A.D.*

Note: "**A Day of Parables**"—Because the Savior told so many parables on this day, it is frequently referred to as "a day of parables."

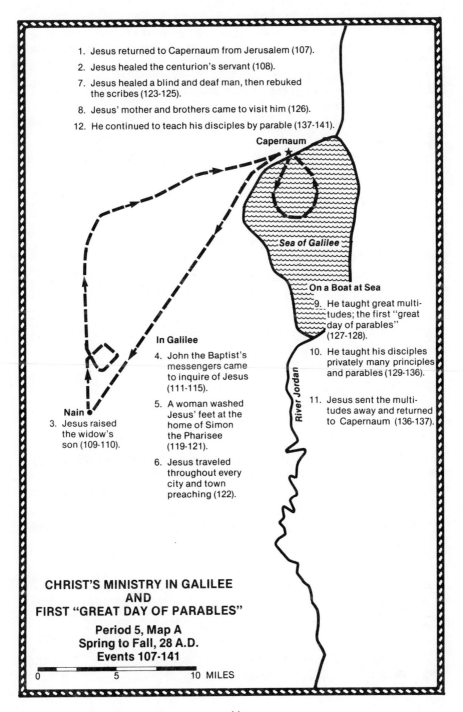

1. Jesus returned to Capernaum from Jerusalem (107).

2. Jesus healed the centurion's servant (108).

7. Jesus healed a blind and deaf man, then rebuked the scribes (123-125).

8. Jesus' mother and brothers came to visit him (126).

12. He continued to teach his disciples by parable (137-141).

Capernaum

Sea of Galilee

On a Boat at Sea

9. He taught great multitudes; the first "great day of parables" (127-128).

10. He taught his disciples privately many principles and parables (129-136).

11. Jesus sent the multitudes away and returned to Capernaum (136-137).

In Galilee

4. John the Baptist's messengers came to inquire of Jesus (111-115).

5. A woman washed Jesus' feet at the home of Simon the Pharisee (119-121).

6. Jesus traveled throughout every city and town preaching (122).

River Jordan

Nain

3. Jesus raised the widow's son (109-110).

**CHRIST'S MINISTRY IN GALILEE
AND
FIRST "GREAT DAY OF PARABLES"**

**Period 5, Map A
Spring to Fall, 28 A.D.
Events 107-141**

0   5   10 MILES

41

129. Jesus told his disciples why he spoke in parables: "I speak to them in parables, because they seeing see not; and hearing they hear not, neither do they understand" **(Mt. 13:10-17; Mk. 4:10-12; Lk. 8:9-10).** *To other disciples and the Twelve when they were alone with Jesus; on a boat(?), Sea of Galilee; the same day(?), Fall, 28 A.D. [★ —Major Discourse #9, Mt. 13:3-52; Mk. 4:3-32; Lk. 8:5-18]*

130. Jesus interpreted the parable of the sower (Mt. 13:18-23; Mk. 4:13-20; Lk. 8:11-15). *(An aside to other disciples and the Twelve when they were alone with Jesus) on a boat(?), Sea of Galilee; the same day, Fall, 28 A.D. ★*

131. Jesus told the parable of the candle under the bushel (Mk. 4:21-25; Lk. 8:16-18). [Compare Mt. 5:14-16) *On a boat, Sea of Galilee; the same day, Fall, 28 A.D. ★*

132. Jesus told the parable of the seed growing secretly (Mk. 4:26-29). *On a boat, Sea of Galilee; the same day, Fall, 28 A.D. ★*

133. Jesus told the parable of the tares of the field (Mt. 13:24-30). *On a boat, Sea of Galilee; the same day, Fall, 28 A.D. ★*

134. Jesus told the parable of the grain of mustard seed (Mt. 13:31-32; Mk. 4:30-32). [Compare Lk. 13:18-19] *On a boat, Sea of Galilee; the same day, Fall, 28 A.D. ★*

135. Jesus told the parable of the hidden leaven (Mt. 13:33). [Compare Lk. 13:20-21] *On a boat, Sea of Galilee; the same day, Fall, 28 A.D. ★*

136. Jesus spoke only in parables to the multitude (Mt. 13:34-35; Mk. 4:33-34). *On a boat, Sea of Galilee; the same day, Fall, 28 A.D.*

137. Jesus sent the multitude away, and went into the house. He explained the parable of the tares of the field to his disciples (Mt. 13:36-43). *In a house, Capernaum(?); the same day, Fall, 28 A.D. ★*

138. Jesus told the parable of the treasure hidden in the field (Mt. 13:44). *In a house, to the disciples, Capernaum(?); the same day, Fall, 28 A.D. ★*

139. Jesus told the parable of the pearl of great price (Mt. 13:45-46). *In a house, to the disciples, Capernaum(?); the same day, Fall, 28 A.D. ★*

140. Jesus told the parable of the net that gathered of every kind (Mt. 13:47-50). *In a house, to the disciples, Capernaum(?); the same day, Fall, 28 A.D. ★*

141. Jesus told the parable of the scribe instructed into the kingdom (Mt. 13:51-52). *In a house, to the disciples, Capernaum(?); the same day, Fall, 28 A.D. ★*

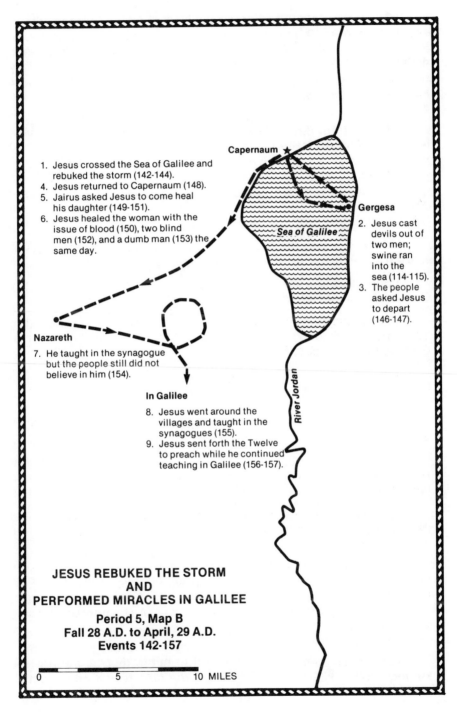

1. Jesus crossed the Sea of Galilee and rebuked the storm (142-144).
4. Jesus returned to Capernaum (148).
5. Jairus asked Jesus to come heal his daughter (149-151).
6. Jesus healed the woman with the issue of blood (150), two blind men (152), and a dumb man (153) the same day.

Capernaum

Gergesa

2. Jesus cast devils out of two men; swine ran into the sea (114-115).
3. The people asked Jesus to depart (146-147).

Sea of Galilee

Nazareth

7. He taught in the synagogue but the people still did not believe in him (154).

In Galilee

8. Jesus went around the villages and taught in the synagogues (155).
9. Jesus sent forth the Twelve to preach while he continued teaching in Galilee (156-157).

River Jordan

**JESUS REBUKED THE STORM
AND
PERFORMED MIRACLES IN GALILEE**

**Period 5, Map B
Fall 28 A.D. to April, 29 A.D.
Events 142-157**

0   5   10 MILES

142. As he prepared to cross the Sea of Galilee, Jesus told a scribe who vowed to follow him, "The Son of man hath not where to lay his head" **(Mt. 8:18-20).** *Capernaum(?); the same day(?), Fall, 28 A.D.*

143. Jesus told a disciple who wished to bury his father, "Follow me, and let the dead bury their dead" **(Mt. 8:21-22).** *Capernaum(?); the same day, Fall, 28 A.D.*

144. Jesus and the disciples crossed the Sea of Galilee; Jesus rebuked the storm (Mk. 4:35-41; Mt. 8:23-27; Lk. 8:22-25). *Crossing west to east, Sea of Galilee; the same day(?), Fall, 28 A.D.*

145. Jesus cast devils out of two men; the devils ran into a herd of swine, which ran into the sea and drowned (Mk. 5:1-13; Lk. 8:26-33; Mt. 8:28-34). *Gergesa; the day after Christ calmed the storm, Fall, 28 A.D.*

Note: **Gergesa and Gadara**—There is confusion in the ancient manuscripts concerning the location of this miracle performed by Jesus. Many believe it actually took place in Gergesa (modern Khersa), near the middle of the east shore of the Sea of Galilee. Gadara is further inland, away from the sea. These very similar names might easily have been confused.

146. The people of Gergesa came to see what had happened, and asked Jesus to depart (Mk. 5:16-17; Lk. 8:34-37; Mt. 8:33-34). *Gergesa; the same day, Fall, 28 A.D.*

147. The man Jesus had healed at Gergesa wanted to go with Jesus, but he said, "Go . . . tell them how great things the Lord hath done for thee, and hath had compassion on thee" **(Mk. 5:18-20; Lk. 8:38-39).** *On board the ship, prior to departure, east coast of the Sea of Galilee; the same day, Fall, 28 A.D.*

148. Jesus and his disciples crossed the Sea of Galilee and returned to Capernaum. People gathered around him near the shore. (Mt. 9:1; Mk. 5:21; Lk. 8:40). *Gergesa to Capernaum; the same day, Fall, 28 A.D.*

149. Jairus, ruler of the synagogue, pleaded with Jesus to come to his house and heal his twelve-year-old daughter. They started toward his house, accompanied by a throng of people (Mk. 5:22-24; Lk. 8:41-42; Mt. 9:18-19). *Capernaum; the same day, Fall, 28 A.D.*

150. As the crowd moved toward Jairus' house, a woman with an issue of blood touched Jesus' robe and was healed. Jesus felt virtue go out of him and told her, "Daughter, be of good comfort: thy faith hath made thee whole; go in peace" **(Mk. 5:25-34; Lk. 8:43-48; Mt. 9:20-22).** *Capernaum; the same day, Fall, 28 A.D.*

151. Jesus took Peter, James, John, and the child's parents, and went into Jairus' house. Though she was dead, Jesus commanded her to arise. Her spirit returned to her body and she arose (Mk. 5:35-43; Lk. 8:49-56; Mt. 9:23-26). *Capernaum; the same day, Fall, 28 A.D.*

152. Jesus came into his own house. Two blind men followed him and Jesus healed them: "According to your faith be it unto you" **(Mt. 9:27-31).** *Jesus' home(?), Capernaum; the same day, Fall, 28 A.D.*

153. Jesus healed a dumb man possessed with a devil (Mt. 9: 32-33). *Jesus' home(?); Capernaum; the same day, Fall, 28 A.D.*

154. Jesus and his disciples went to Nazareth and he taught in the synagogue there. He could do no mighty works there because of their unbelief. "A prophet is not without honor, but in his own country, and among his own kin, and in his own house" **(Mk. 6:1-6; Mt. 13:54-58).** [Compare Lk. 4:16-30] *Capernaum to Nazareth; Winter, 28 A.D.*

155. Jesus went around the villages teaching in their synagogues, and preaching the gospel of the kingdom. Jesus was moved with compassion because the multitudes lacked leadership: "The harvest truly is plenteous, but the laborers are few" **(Mt. 9:35-38).** *Galilee; Winter, 29 A.D.*

156. Jesus sent forth his twelve apostles, two by two, to preach (Mk. 6:7-13; Lk. 9:1-6). [Compare Mt. 10:1-42] *Unknown location, Galilee; Winter, 28 A.D.* ★

157. Jesus continued to teach and preach in the cities of Galilee (Mt. 11:1). *Galilee; Winter, 29 A.D.*

158. Herod (the tetrarch) held a feast. Salome (the daughter of Herodias) danced for him. In answer to her request, Herod had John the Baptist beheaded (Mk. 6:17-29; Mt. 14:3-12). *Herod's palace: Tiberias, on the Sea of Galilee; John's prison: Fortress of Machaerus; Winter, 29 A.D.*

159. Herod (the tetrarch)) heard of Jesus, wondered if he was John the Baptist risen from the dead, and desired to see him (Mk. 6:14-16; Lk. 9:7-9; Mt. 14:1-2). *Herod's palace: Tiberias, on the Sea of Galilee; Winter, 29 A.D.*

160. The Twelve returned from their missions and reported to Jesus (Mk. 6:30; Lk. 9:10). Unknown location, Galilee; Winter, 29 A.D.

161. The disciples of John the Baptist reported John's death to Jesus (Mt. 14:12). *Unknown location, Galilee; April, 29 A.D.*

162. Jesus and his disciples went by ship to a secluded desert place near Bethsaida (Lk. 9:10; Mk. 6:31-32; Mt. 14:13). *Near (probably east of) Bethsaida Julias, Galilee; April, 29 A.D.*

163. People from the nearby cities outran Jesus' boat, and were there waiting for Jesus when he landed. He had compassion on them, taught them of the kingdom of God, and healed them (Mk. 6:33-34; Lk. 9:11; Mt. 14:14). *Desert ot seashore near Bethsaida Julias, Galilee; April, 29 A.D.*

164. Jesus miraculously multiplied loaves of bread and fishes, and fed five thousand men, plus women and children (Jn. 6:1-14; Mk. 6:35-44; Mt. 14:14-21; Lk. 9:11-17). *On a mountain near Bethsaida Julius, Galilee; evening of the same day, shortly before the (3rd) Passover, April, 29 A.D.*

165. Jesus instructed his disciples to sail to the other side of Bethsaida while he sent away the people. He prevented a move by the people to make him a king (Mk. 6:45-46; Mt. 14:22-23; Jn. 6:15). *Near Bethsaida Julius, Galilee; evening of the same day, April, 29 A.D.*

166. Jesus went alone to a mountain to pray (Mk. 6:46; Mt. 14:23; Jn. 6:15). *Near Bethsaida Julius, Galilee; night of the same day, April, 29 A.D.*

167. A fierce storm arose as his disciples rowed through the night. Jesus walked on the sea and joined them in the ship. Peter walked on the water to meet him. As they entered the ship the wind ceased and they found themselves close to land (Mt. 14:24-33; Mk. 6:47-52; Jn. 6:16-21). *On the sea near Julius Bethsaida, probably crossing east to west, they rowed from 3 to 3½ miles (1 furlong = 220 yards); the same night, during fourth watch (3-6 a.m.), April, 29 A.D.*

168. The multitude sought Jesus in Capernaum, but found him on the plain of Gennesaret (Jn. 6:22-25; Mt. 14:34; Mk. 6:53). *Gennesaret plain, Galilee; the next day, April, 29 A.D.*

Note: The Plain of Gennesaret—This plain extends southward from Capernaum, on the west side of the Sea of Galilee. It is extremely fertile, producing grapes and figs and other fruits almost all year round. It has been termed "a garden of princes" and "a paradise."

169. The people from the Gennesaret area came to see Jesus, and many were healed just by touching the hem of his robe (Mk. 6:54-56; Mt. 14:35-36). *Gennesaret Plain; the same day, April, 29 A.D.*

170. When the multitude inquired how Jesus came to be with his disciples (whom they knew had sailed without him), Jesus preached to them, declaring himself to be the bread of life: "He that believeth on me hath everlasting life. I am that bread of life" **(Jn. 6:25-59).** *Synagogue at Capernaum; the same day(?), April 29 A.D.* **[★ —Major Discourse #10]**

171. Many of Jesus' disciples, offended by Jesus' "bread-of-life" sermon and his explanation of it, left and walked no more with him (Jn. 6:60-66). *Capernaum; the same day, April, 29 A.D.* ★

Note: Jesus' Popularity During His Ministry—This event marked the beginning of the falling away of Jesus' following. Some commentators have described his ministry as having varying characteristics during various periods. The early Judean ministry has been termed the *period of obscurity;* most of his Galilean ministry has been called the *period of popularity;* his Perean ministry has been called the *period of opposition;* and the post-resurrection period has been termed the *period of triumph.* Most of his following came from the north (Galilee); most of his opposition came from the south (Judea).

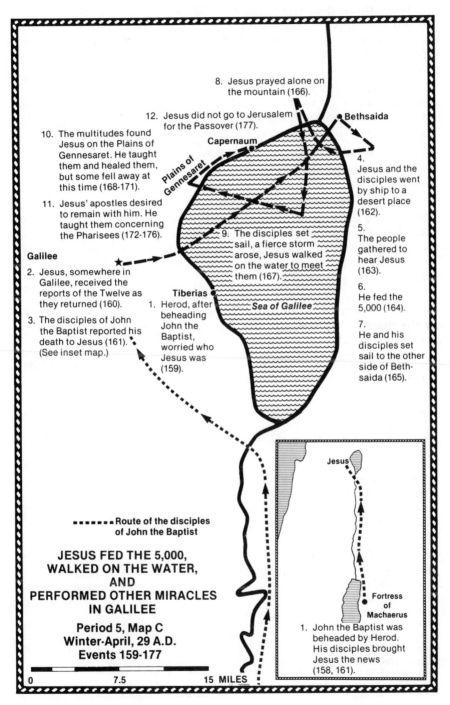

8. Jesus prayed alone on the mountain (166).

12. Jesus did not go to Jerusalem for the Passover (177).

Bethsaida

Capernaum

10. The multitudes found Jesus on the Plains of Gennesaret. He taught them and healed them, but some fell away at this time (168-171).

11. Jesus' apostles desired to remain with him. He taught them concerning the Pharisees (172-176).

Plains of Gennesaret

4. Jesus and the disciples went by ship to a desert place (162).

5. The people gathered to hear Jesus (163).

Galilee

2. Jesus, somewhere in Galilee, received the reports of the Twelve as they returned (160).

3. The disciples of John the Baptist reported his death to Jesus (161). (See inset map.)

9. The disciples set sail, a fierce storm arose, Jesus walked on the water to meet them (167).

Tiberias

1. Herod, after beheading John the Baptist, worried who Jesus was (159).

Sea of Galilee

6. He fed the 5,000 (164).

7. He and his disciples set sail to the other side of Bethsaida (165).

- - - - - - Route of the disciples of John the Baptist

JESUS FED THE 5,000, WALKED ON THE WATER, AND PERFORMED OTHER MIRACLES IN GALILEE

Period 5, Map C
Winter-April, 29 A.D.
Events 159-177

0   7.5   15 MILES

Jesus

Fortress of Machaerus

1. John the Baptist was beheaded by Herod. His disciples brought Jesus the news (158, 161).

47

172. Jesus gave the twelve an opportunity to leave his service, but they remained, asserting: "We believe and are sure that thou art that Christ, the Son of the living God" **(Jn. 6:67-71).** *Capernaum; the same day, April, 29 A.D.*

173. Jesus rebuked a group of scribes and Pharisees from Jerusalem, who complained that his disciples ate with unwashed hands: "Laying aside the commandment of God, ye hold the tradition of men" **(Mk. 7:1-13; Mt. 15:1-9).** *Capernaum(?), April, 29 A.D.* ★

174. Jesus called the nearby people together and expounded the principle of cleanliness he had discussed with the scribes and Pharisees: "Not that which goeth into the mouth defileth a man; but that which cometh out of the mouth, this defileth a man" **(Mt. 15:10-11; Mk. 7:14-16).** *Capernaum(?); April, 29 A.D.* ★

175. Jesus commented to his disciples concerning the Pharisees: "They be blind leaders of the blind. And if the blind lead the blind, both shall fall into the ditch" **(Mt. 15:12-14).** In a house, in Capernaum(?); the same day, April, 29 A.D.

176. Jesus further explained the doctrine of cleanliness to his disciples, privately: "From within, out of the heart of men, proceed evil thoughts, adulteries, fornications, murders, . . ." **(Mk. 7:17-23; Mt. 15:15-20).** *In a house, in Capernaum(?); the same day, April, 29 A.D.* ★

177. The third Passover celebration during Christ's ministry was held, but Jesus did not attend the Jerusalem celebration. *April, 29 A.D.*

JEWISH MEASURES OF WEIGHT, LENGTH AND DISTANCE

	Avoirdupois			Troy			
	lbs.	oz.	drs.	lbs.	oz.	dwt.	grs.
A gerah	—	—	.439 =	—	—	—	12
10 gerahs = 1 bekah	—	—	4.39 =	—	—	5	0
2 bekahs = 1 shekel	—	—	8.9 =	—	—	10	0
60 shekels = 1 maneh	.2	0	14.628 =	.2	6	0	0
50 manehs = 1 talent	10.2	13	11.428 =	12.5	0	0	0

SHORTER MEASURES OF LENGTH

		FT.	IN.
A digit, or finger (Jer. 52:21).............		—	0.912
4 digits	= 1 palm (Ex. 25:25)	—	3.648
3 palms	= 1 span (Ex. 28:16)	—	10.944
2 spans	= 1 cubit (Gen. 6:15)	1	9.888
4 cubits	= 1 fathom (Acts 27:28)	7	3.552
1.5 fathoms = 1 reed (Ezek. 40:3, 5)		10	11.328
13.3 reeds	= 1 line (Ezek. 40:3)	145	11.04

LONGER MEASURES OF DISTANCE

	Eng. miles	paces	ft.
A cubit	—	1.824	
400 cubits = 1 furlong (Lk. 24:13)	—	145	4.6
10 furlongs = 1 mile (Mt. 5:41)	1	403	1.0
15 furlongs = 1 Sabbath-day's journey (Jn. 11:18; Acts 1:12)	2	132	4.0
24 miles	= 1 day's journey..................................	33	172	4.0

Period 6

CHRIST'S LATE GALILEAN MINISTRY

(From Christ's Visit to Phoenicia to the Feast of Tabernacles in Jerusalem)

April, 29 A.D. to October, 29 A.D.

Matthew 15:21-18:35   Luke 9:18-10:16
Mark 7:24-9:50   John 7:1-10

Jesus Visited Tyre, Sidon, and Decapolis
Jesus Fed the Four Thousand
Peter's Testimony of Christ
The Transfiguration of Jesus
The Fish with Tribute Money in its Mouth
Jesus Taught About the Meekness of Little Children

178. Jesus and his disciples went to Tyre and Sidon, because the Jews sought to kill him (Mt. 15:21; Mk. 7:24; Jn. 7:1). *Capernaum to Tyre and Sidon; Spring-Summer, 29 A.D.*

Note: **Tyre and Sidon**—Tyre was a major Phoenician port city which was larger than Jerusalem in New Testament times. It was first built on the mainland, then rebuilt on a nearby island. It was powerful as a merchant city and was especially famous for the metalwork, glassware and dyes which were produced there.

Sidon was another wealthy city of Phoenicia, located less than 20 miles north of Tyre on the Mediterranean seacoast, and about 50 miles north of Nazareth.

179. A Syrophoenician woman came to the house where Jesus was in seclusion, and asked Jesus to cast the devil out of her daughter. The girl was healed: "O woman, great is thy faith: be it unto thee even as thou wilt" **(Mt. 15:22-28; Mk. 7:24-30).** *Near Sidon(?); Summer, 29 A.D.*

Note: **Syro-Phoenicia**—The native name for Phoenicia was *Kenaan* (Canaan), meaning "lowland," as contrasted with the adjoining *Aram,* or highland (the Hebrew name for Syria). The area was a coastal plain about 28 miles long, with a width of 2 to 5 miles between the sea and the mountains to the east. The Greeks gave the area the name *Phoenicia,* meaning "palm tree." At the time of Christ, the area was part of

49

the Roman province of Syria, so its inhabitants were, at the same time, Canaanites, Syrians, and Phoenicians.

180. Jesus left Phoenicia, traveled through Decapolis, and came to a mountain near the Sea of Galilee (Mk. 7:31; Mt. 15:29). *Phoenicia to Decapolis to the Sea of Galilee; Summer, 29 A.D.*

Note: Decapolis—This area was a league of 10 independent cities (later increased to 18), inhabited by Greeks who had come in the wake of Alexander's conquest. The alliance was established after the Romans occupied the area in 65 B.C. They had their own army, coinage and courts.

181. A great multitude came to see Jesus on the mountain and remained with him for three days. Jesus healed their sick (Mt. 15:30-32). *On a mountain near the Sea of Galilee (Near Bethsaida Julias?); Summer, 29 A.D.*

182. Jesus privately healed a deaf man with a speech impediment (Mk. 7:32-37). *On a mountain near the Sea of Galilee; during the three days(?), Summer, 29 A.D.*

183. Jesus miraculously multiplied loaves and fishes and fed four thousand men, plus women and children (Mk. 8:1-9; Mt. 15:32-38). [Compare Mt. 14:14-21; Mk. 6:33-44; Lk. 9:11-17; and Jn. 6:1-14] *On a mountain near the Sea of Galilee; after the three days, Summer, 29 A.D.*

184. Jesus sent away the multitude, and sailed to Magdala (Mt. 15:39; Mk. 8:10). *Magdala (Dalmanutha, mentioned in Mark, is unknown); Summer, 29 A.D.*

185. The Pharisees and Sadducees came to Jesus, seeking a sign, but Jesus told them no sign would be given but the sign of the prophet Jonah: "A wicked and adulterous generation seeketh after a sign . . ." **(Mt. 16:1-4; Mk. 8:11-13).** *Magdala; Summer, 29 A.D.*

186. Jesus and his disciples sailed across the Sea of Galilee to Bethsaida (Mk. 8:13; Mt. 16:5). *Magdala to Bethsaida; the same day, Summer, 29 A.D.*

187. While on board the ship, Jesus warned his disciples of the Pharisees, of the Sadducees, and of Herod (Mk. 8:14-21; Mt. 16:5-12). *On board ship, Magdala to Bethsaida; the same day while sailing, Summer, 29 A.D.* ★

188. Jesus healed a blind man in Bethsaida (Mk. 8:22-26). *Bethsaida Julius; Summer, 29 A.D.*

189. Jesus and his disciples visited the area of Caesarea Philippi (Mk. 8:27; Mt. 16:13). *Bethsaida to Caesarea Philippi; Summer or Fall, 29 A.D.*

Note: Caesarea Philippi—This town stands 1150 feet above sea level, near the foot of Mt. Hermon (9,000 feet), in the area where the Jordan River originates. It is not the same town as Caesarea (Caesarea Palestina), the coastal city which served as the headquarters for Pontius Pilate. Philip, son of Herod the Great, rebuilt this city, changed its name from Paneas, and made it his capital of Palestine's northeast districts which he governed.

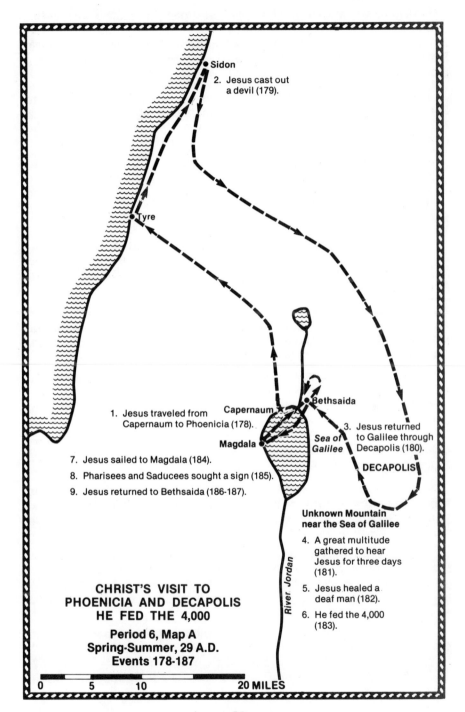

Sidon

2. Jesus cast out a devil (179).

Tyre

1. Jesus traveled from Capernaum to Phoenicia (178).

7. Jesus sailed to Magdala (184).

8. Pharisees and Saducees sought a sign (185).

9. Jesus returned to Bethsaida (186-187).

Capernaum

Bethsaida

Magdala

Sea of Galilee

3. Jesus returned to Galilee through Decapolis (180).

DECAPOLIS

Unknown Mountain near the Sea of Galilee

4. A great multitude gathered to hear Jesus for three days (181).

5. Jesus healed a deaf man (182).

6. He fed the 4,000 (183).

River Jordan

CHRIST'S VISIT TO PHOENICIA AND DECAPOLIS HE FED THE 4,000

**Period 6, Map A
Spring-Summer, 29 A.D.
Events 178-187**

0   5   10   20 MILES

190. Jesus asked his disciples who people said he was. Peter replied: "Thou art the Christ, the Son of the living God." **Jesus blessed Peter and gave him the "keys of the kingdom of heaven" (Mt. 16:13-20; Mk. 8:27-30; Lk. 9:18-21).** *Near Caesarea Philippi; while Jesus was alone praying with his disciples, Summer or Fall, 29 A.D.* ★

191. Jesus began to show his disciples how he would go to Jerusalem to be captured, killed, and raised again (Mt. 16:21-22; Mk. 8:31; Lk. 9:22). *Near Caesarea Philippi; the same day, Summer or Fall, 29 A.D.*

192. Peter spoke words he thought were in Jesus' defense, but Jesus rebuked him: "Get thee behind me, Satan; thou art an offence unto me: for thou savourest not the things that be of God, but those that be of men" **(Mt. 16:22-23; Mk. 8:32-33).** *Near Caesarea Philippi; the same day, Summer or Fall, 29 A.D.*

193. Jesus taught the people and his disciples, "Whosoever will come after me, let him deny himself, and take up his cross, and follow me" **(Mk. 8:34-38; Mt. 16:24-27; Lk. 9:23-26).** *Near Caesarea Philippi; the same day, Summer or Fall, 29 A.D.*

194. Jesus prophesied, "There be some standing here, which shall not taste of death, till they see the Son of Man coming in his kingdom" **(Mt. 16:28; Mk. 9:1; Lk. 9:27).** [Compare Jn. 21:22-23] *Near Caesarea Philippi; the same day, Summer or Fall, 29 A.D.*

195. Jesus took Peter, James, and John up into a high mountain and was transfigured before them. Moses and Elias [Elijah] appeared and talked to him. A bright cloud appeared and a voice said, "This is my beloved Son, in whom I am well pleased; hear ye him." **(Mt. 17:1-9; Lk. 9:28-36; Mk. 9:2-10).** *On a high mountain near Caesarea Philippi, presumably Mt. Hermon; six days later, at night(?), Summer or Fall, 29 A.D.* ★

196. Jesus explained to Peter, James and John that John the Baptist had come and functioned in the role of an Elias [forerunner] (Mt. 17:10-13; Mk. 9:11-13). *While descending Mt. Hermon(?); the same day, Summer or Fall, 29 A.D.*

197. When they came back to the multitude, Jesus healed a man's lunatic son, whom his disciples had been unable to cure: "If thou canst believe, all things are possible to him that believeth" **(Mk. 9:14-27; Mt. 17:14-18; Lk. 9:37-42).** *Near Caesarea Philippi; the next day, Summer or Fall, 29 A.D.*

198. Jesus explained to his disciples why they could not cast out the evil spirit in the lunatic boy: "Because of your unbelief: . . . howbeit this kind goeth not out but by prayer and fasting" **(Mt. 17: 19-21; Mk. 9:28-29).** *In a house, near Caesarea Philippi; the same day(?), Summer or Fall, 29 A.D.*

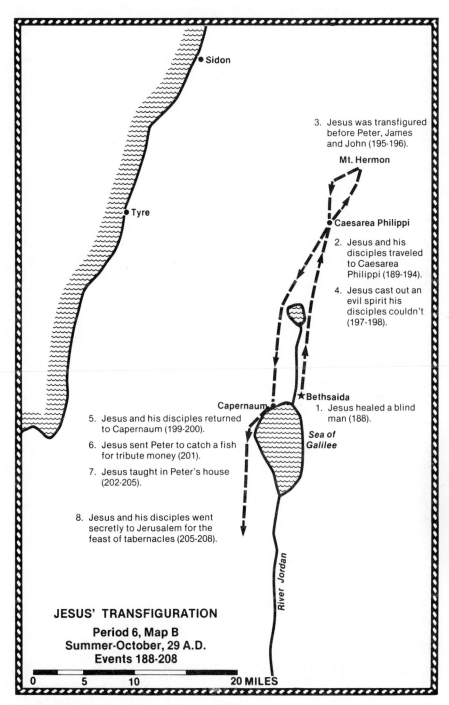

Sidon

3. Jesus was transfigured
   before Peter, James
   and John (195-196).

Mt. Hermon

Tyre

Caesarea Philippi

2. Jesus and his
   disciples traveled
   to Caesarea
   Philippi (189-194).

4. Jesus cast out an
   evil spirit his
   disciples couldn't
   (197-198).

★Bethsaida

Capernaum

1. Jesus healed a blind
   man (188).

5. Jesus and his disciples returned
   to Capernaum (199-200).

*Sea of
Galilee*

6. Jesus sent Peter to catch a fish
   for tribute money (201).

7. Jesus taught in Peter's house
   (202-205).

8. Jesus and his disciples went
   secretly to Jerusalem for the
   feast of tabernacles (205-208).

River Jordan

JESUS' TRANSFIGURATION

**Period 6, Map B
Summer-October, 29 A.D.
Events 188-208**

0   5   10   20 MILES

53

199. Jesus and his disciples passed through Galilee to Capernaum without anyone knowing of their presence (Mk. 9:30). *Caesarea Philippi to Capernaum; Summer or Fall, 29 A.D.*

200. Jesus taught his disciples that he would be betrayed, killed, and that he would rise again the third day (Mk. 9:31-32; Mt. 17:22-23; Lk. 9:43-45). *Enroute from Caesarea Philippi to Capernaum; Summer or Fall, 29 A.D.*

201. Tax collectors sought tribute from Jesus, who sent Peter to catch a fish, telling him that the first fish he caught would have a piece of money in its mouth to serve as tribute (Mt. 17:24-27). *Capernaum; Summer or Fall, 29 A.D.*

202. To answer his disciples' question concerning who was greatest in the kingdom of God, Jesus used a little child as an example, and taught them of meekness, offenses and sealing power: "Except ye be converted, and become as little children, ye shall not enter into the kingdom of heaven." *Parable:* The Lost Sheep (Mt. 18: 12-14). **(Mt. 18:1-20; Mk. 9:33-37, 42-50; Lk. 9:46-48).** *In "the" house at Capernaum; Summer or Fall, 29 A.D. [★ —Major Discourse #11, Mt. 18:1-35; Mk. 9:35-50]*

203. Jesus answered John's question about a man who was not a disciple who cast out devils in Jesus' name: "Forbid him not: for he that is not against us is for us" **(Mk. 9:38-41; Lk. 9:49-50).** *In "the" house at Capernaum; the same day, Summer or Fall, 29 A.D. ★*

204. Jesus answered Peter's questions about how often one must forgive another: "I say not unto thee, Until seven times: but, Until seventy times seven" *Parable:* The Unmerciful Servant **(Mt. 18:21-35).** *In the house at Capernaum; the same day, Summer ◦ Fall, 29 A.D. ★*

205. Jesus prepared to go to Jerusalem. The messengers he sent to prepare the way were turned away by the Samaritans. When James and John wanted to call down fire upon them, Jesus rebuked them, saying "The Son of man is not come to de ·troy men's lives, but to save them" **(Lk. 9:51-56).** *Messengers: Capernaum to Samaria to Capernaum; Summer or Fall, 29 A.D.*

206. Jesus' instructions to those who wished to follow him: "No man, having put his hand to the plough, and looking back, is fit for the kingdom of God" **(Lk. 9:57-62).** [Compare Mt. 8:19-22] *Near Capernaum, Summer or Fall, 29 A.D.*

207. Jesus' brethren urged him to go to the feast of tabernacles, but he declined: "The world cannot hate you; but me it hateth, because I testify of it, that the works thereof are evil" **(Jn. 7:2-9).** *Galilee; Summer or Fall, 29 A.D.*

208. Jesus went in secret to the feast of tabernacles in Jerusalem (Jn. 7:10). *Galilee to Jerusalem; Oct., 29 A.D.*

Period 7

CHRIST'S LATE JUDEAN MINISTRY

(From The Feast of Tabernacles to The Feast of the Dedication)

October, 29 A.D. to December, 29 A.D.

Luke 10:1-13:22　　　John 7:11-10:39

Jesus Taught in the Temple at the Feast of Tabernacles
Jesus Healed a Blind Man Whom the Pharisees Questioned
Jesus Taught the Pharisees He Was the Door to the Kingdom
Jesus Sent the Seventy Forth to Preach
Jesus Told the Lawyer How to Gain Eternal Life
Jesus Visited Mary and Martha
Jesus Ate with a Pharisee and Reproved the Pharisees and Lawyers
Jesus Escaped Stoning at the Feast of the Dedication

209. The Jews sought Jesus at the feast of tabernacles, but his followers dared not speak of him openly (Jn. 7:11-13). *Jerusalem; during the feast of tabernacles, Oct. 11-18, 29 A.D.*

Note: **The Feast of Tabernacles**—This feast commemorated the entrance of the Israelites into the promised land after their wandering in the wilderness. It fell in the fall, and lasted for eight days (Lev. 23:34-46; Deut. 16:13-15). It began five days after the Day of Atonement (Lev. 23:27). This was fifteen days after the feast of trumpets, which was held on the first day of the seventh month (October), and began the Jewish civil year (Lev. 23:24). During the festival, the Jews were to dwell in booths or huts made of tree branches, to remind them of the huts lived in by the wandering Israelites.

210. Jesus taught in the temple during the feast of tabernacles, testifying that he was sent of the Father: "If any man will do his will,

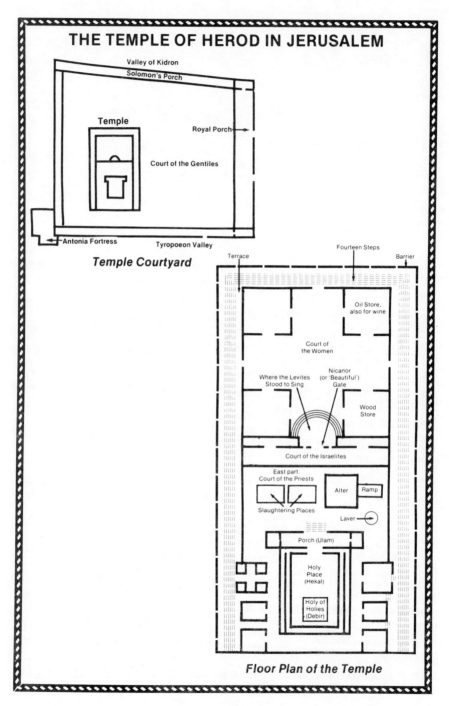

THE TEMPLE OF HEROD IN JERUSALEM

Temple Courtyard

Floor Plan of the Temple

he shall know of the doctrine, whether it be of God, or whether I speak of myself" **(Jn. 7:14-31).** *Temple of Herod, Jerusalem; about Oct. 15, 29 A.D. [★ —Major Discourse #12, Jn. 7:16-39]*

211. The Pharisees and chief priests sent officers to the temple to arrest Jesus (Jn. 7:32). *Jerusalem; during the feast of tabernacles, Oct. 11-18, 29 A.D.*

212. Jesus preached on the last day of the feast of tabernacles: "If any man thirst, let him come unto me, and drink" **(Jn. 7:37-39).** *Temple of Herod, Jerusalem; Oct. 18, 29 A.D.* ★

213. The people debated whether Jesus was the Christ (Jn. 7:40-44). *Temple of Herod, Jerusalem; after the feast of tabernacles, Oct., 29 A.D.*

214. The chief priests and the Pharisees rebuked the officers for not arresting Jesus (Jn. 7:45-49). *Jerusalem; after the feast of tabernacles, Oct., 29 A.D.*

215. Nicodemus spoke to the chief priests in defense of Jesus: "Doth our law judge any man, before it heareth him, and know what he doeth?" **(Jn. 7:50-53).** *Jerusalem; after the feast of tabernacles, Oct., 29 A.D.*

216. Jesus went to the Mount of Olives (Jn. 8:1). *Outside Jerusalem; after the feast of tabernacles, Oct., 29 A.D.*

217. Jesus taught in the temple. When the scribes and Pharisees brought unto him a woman taken in adultery he said, "He that is without sin among you, let him first cast a stone at her" **(Jn. 8:2-11).** *Temple of Herod, Jerusalem; early in the morning, after the feast of tabernacles, Oct., 29 A.D.*

218. Jesus preached to the Pharisees who challenged him in the temple, until they attempted to stone him: "I am the light of the world: he that followeth me shall not walk in darkness, but shall have the light of life" **(Jn. 8:12-59).** *Temple of Herod, Jerusalem; the same day, after the feast of tabernacles, Oct., 29 A.D. [★ —Major Discourse #13]*

219. Jesus healed a man born blind, and sent him to wash in the pool of Siloam. He told his disciples the man was born blind "that the works of God should be made manifest in him" **(Jn. 9:1-12).** *Near the pool of Siloam, Jerusalem; after the feast of tabernacles, Oct., 29 A.D.*

220. The Pharisees questioned the blind man Jesus had healed, rejecting the miracle because the healing took place on the Sabbath. (Jn. 9:13-17). *Jerusalem; after the feast of tabernacles, Oct., 29 A.D.*

221. The Pharisees interviewed the parents of the blind man Jesus healed, who told them only that the man was born blind (Jn. 9:18-23). *Jerusalem; the same day(?), after the feast of tabernacles, Oct., 29 A.D.*

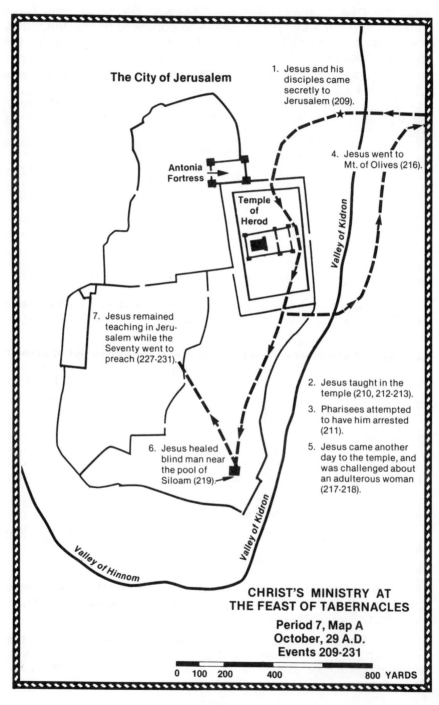

The City of Jerusalem

1. Jesus and his disciples came secretly to Jerusalem (209).

4. Jesus went to Mt. of Olives (216).

Antonia Fortress

Temple of Herod

Valley of Kidron

7. Jesus remained teaching in Jerusalem while the Seventy went to preach (227-231).

2. Jesus taught in the temple (210, 212-213).

3. Pharisees attempted to have him arrested (211).

5. Jesus came another day to the temple, and was challenged about an adulterous woman (217-218).

6. Jesus healed blind man near the pool of Siloam (219).

Valley of Kidron

Valley of Hinnom

CHRIST'S MINISTRY AT THE FEAST OF TABERNACLES

**Period 7, Map A
October, 29 A.D.
Events 209-231**

0 100 200   400   800 YARDS

222. The Pharisees again interviewed the blind man Jesus healed. When the blind man began to comment on doctrine, they cast him out (Jn. 9:24-34). *Jerusalem; the same day(?), after the feast of tabernacles, Oct., 29 A.D.* ★

223. Jesus found the blind man he had healed. When the man asked who was the Son of God, Jesus told him: "Thou hast both seen him, and it is he that talketh with thee" **(Jn. 9:35-38).** *Jerusalem; the same day(?), after the feast of tabernacles, Oct., 29 A.D.* ★

224. Jesus told the Pharisees their sins remained with them, and said, "For judgment I am come into this world, that they which see not might see, and they which see might be made blind" **(Jn. 9:39-41).** *Jerusalem; the same day, after the feast of tabernacles, Oct., 29 A.D.* ★

225. Jesus taught the Pharisees that he was the door by which the sheep must enter God's kingdom: "I am the good shepherd: the good shepherd giveth his life for the sheep." *Parable:* Entering the Sheepfold **(Jn. 10:1-18).** *Jerusalem; the same day, after the feast of tabernacles, Oct., 29 A.D. [* ★ *—Major Discourse #14]*

226. The Pharisees disputed whether Jesus was mad or had a devil (Jn. 10:19-21). *Jerusalem; the same day, after the feast of tabernacles, Oct., 29 A.D.*

227. Jesus appointed the seventy, and sent them out to preach: "Pray ye therefore the Lord of the harvest, that he would send forth laborers into his harvest" **(Lk. 10:1-16).** [Compare Mt. 10:7-42; 11:20-24] *Jerusalem(?); in connection with the feast of tabernacles(?), Oct., 29 A.D.*

Note: **Time of the Mission of the Seventy**—Difficulty exists in correlating the chronology of the sending forth and return of the seventy (Lk. 10:1-17) with Jesus' visit to Jerusalem for the feast of tebernacles (Jn. 7:2-10-21). If the call and return of the seventy preceded Jesus' journey to Jerusalem, then they must have left from and returned to Galilee (Capernaum?) and the account should have been classified as part of Period #6, Christ's Late Galilean Ministry. If Jesus called the seventy to labor in Judea, he probably called them from Jerusalem, about the time of the feast of tabernacles. The latter approach is followed here.

228. The seventy returned from their preaching with joy, and Jesus told them: "Rejoice, because your names are written in heaven" **(Lk. 10:17-20).** *Jerusalem(?); late Fall, 29 A.D.*

229. Jesus prayed and gave thanks to his Father: "All things are delivered to me of my Father" **(Lk. 10:21-22).** [Compare Mt. 11:25-27] *Jerusalem(?); the same day in that hour, late Fall, 29 A.D.*

230. Jesus told his disciples they were blessed to see the things which they were seeing: "Many prophets have desired to see those things which ye see, and have not seen them" **(Lk. 10:23-24).** *Jerusalem(?); the same day, late Fall, 29 A.D.*

231. Jesus replied to the lawyer who asked "What shall I do to inherit eternal life? . . . Thou shalt love the Lord thy God with all thy heart, . . . and thy neighbor as thyself." *Parable:* The Good Samaritan **(Lk. 10:25-37).** *Jerusalem(?) or near Bethany(?), late Fall, 29 A.D.*

232. Jesus visited Mary and Martha in Bethany (Lk. 10:38-42). *Bethany; late Fall, 29 A.D.*

233. Jesus taught his disciples how to pray, and again gave them the Lord's Prayer (Lk. 11:1-13). [Compare Mt. 6:9-13, 7:7-11] *Judea; late Fall, 29 A.D.* ★

234. Jesus cast a devil out of a man who was dumb. When accused of casting out devils through Beelzebub, he rebuked them, saying "If I by Beelzebub cast out devils, by whom do your sons cast them out?" **(Lk. 11:14-26).** [Compare Mt. 12:24-45] *Judea; late Fall, 29 A.D. [★ —Major Discourse #15, Lk. 11:17-52]*

235. A woman of the company lifted her voice and said, "Blessed is the womb that bare thee." **Jesus replied,** "Yea rather, blessed are they that hear the word of God, and keep it" **(Lk. 11:27-28).** *Judea; the same day, while Jesus was reproving his critics, late Fall, 29 A.D.*

236. Jesus reproved the Pharisees: "When thine eye is evil, thy body also is full of darkness. Take heed therefore that the light which is in thee be not darkness" **(Lk. 11:29-36).** *Judea; the same day, while Jesus was reproving his critics, late Fall, 29 A.D.* ★

237. Jesus went to dinner with a Pharisee, who was critical of Jesus for not washing his hands. Jesus criticized the Pharisees: "Ye Pharisees make clean the outside of the cup and the platter; but your inward part is full of ravening and wickedness" **(Lk. 11:37-44).** [Compare Mk. 7:1-13] *Judea; the same day, late Fall, 29 A.D.* ★

238. Jesus criticized lawyers: "Ye lade men with burdens grievous to be borne, and ye yourselves touch not the burdens with one of your fingers" **(Lk. 11:45-52).** *Judea, the same day, while eating with the Pharisees, late Fall, 29 A.D.* ★

239. The scribes and Pharisees urged Jesus on, provoking him to speak of many things, seeking for something with which to accuse him (Lk. 11:53-54). *Judea; the same day, while eating with the Pharisees, late Fall, 29 A.D.*

240. Jesus instructed an innumerable multitude: "Seek ye the kingdom of God; and all these things shall be added unto you" **(Lk. 12:1-59)** [Compare Mt. 6, 7] *Parables:* The Foolish Rich Man; The Faithful and Wise Steward. *Judea; late Fall, 29 A.D. [★ —Major Discourse #16]*

241. Jesus was told of Galileans who had been slain by Pilate. He explained that untimely death is not the result of sin. *Parable:* The Barren Fig Tree **(Lk. 13:1-10).** *In a synagogue, Judea; on the Sabbath, late Fall, 29 A.D.*

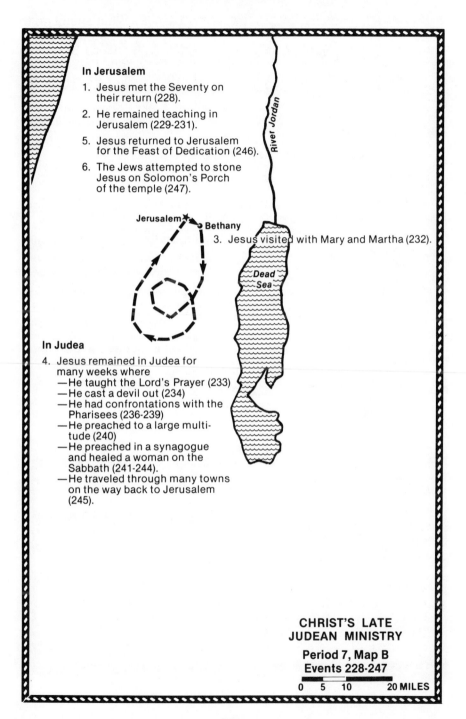

In Jerusalem

1. Jesus met the Seventy on their return (228).

2. He remained teaching in Jerusalem (229-231).

5. Jesus returned to Jerusalem for the Feast of Dedication (246).

6. The Jews attempted to stone Jesus on Solomon's Porch of the temple (247).

Jerusalem

Bethany

3. Jesus visited with Mary and Martha (232).

River Jordan

Dead Sea

In Judea

4. Jesus remained in Judea for many weeks where
   —He taught the Lord's Prayer (233)
   —He cast a devil out (234)
   —He had confrontations with the Pharisees (236-239)
   —He preached to a large multitude (240)
   —He preached in a synagogue and healed a woman on the Sabbath (241-244).
   —He traveled through many towns on the way back to Jerusalem (245).

**CHRIST'S LATE
JUDEAN MINISTRY**

**Period 7, Map B
Events 228-247**

0   5   10   20 MILES

242. Jesus healed a woman who had been bowed over for 18 years: "Woman, thou art loosed from thine infirmity" **(Lk. 13:11-13).** *In a synagogue, Judea; the same day, late Fall, 29 A.D.*

243. Jesus rebuked the ruler of the synagogue, who criticized him for healing on the Sabbath: "Ought not this woman, . . . whom Satan hath bound, lo, these eighteen years, be loosed from this bond on the Sabbath day?" **(Lk. 13:14-17).** *In a synagogue, Judea; the same day, late Fall, 29 A.D.* ★

244. Jesus made comparisons to the kingdom of God. *Parables:* The Mustard Seed; The Leaven. **(Lk. 13:18-21).** *In a synagogue, Judea; the same day, late Fall, 29 A.D.* ★

245. Jesus went through the cities and villages, teaching, and journeying toward Jerusalem (Lk. 13:22). *Judea; Dec., 29 A.D.*

246. Jesus attended the feast of the dedication at Jerusalem (Jn. 10:22). *Jerusalem; Dec. 25, 29 A.D. - Jan. 1, 30 A.D.*

Note: **The Feast of Dedication**—Judas Maccabaeus instituted this feast in 164 B.C. to commemorate the purification of the temple in Jerusalem which had been profaned by the idolatrous Syrian king Antiochus Epiphanes. It became customary to refer to the feast as "the feast of lights" because of the brilliant illuminations used in the celebration. The feast began on December 25th and lasted for eight days.

247. The Jews attempted to stone Jesus because he told them he was the Son of God: "Say ye of him, whom the Father hath sanctified, and sent into the world, Thou blasphemest; because I said, I am the Son of God?" **(Jn. 10:23-39).** *Solomon's Porch, Temple of Herod, Jerusalem; during the feast of the dedication, late Dec., 29 A.D.*

APPROXIMATE ROAD-MILES FROM JERUSALEM

Amman, 58	Cana, 103	Nazareth, 80
Beersheba, 45	Capernaum, 109	Nablus, 38
Bethany, 2	Damascus, 183	Samaria, 45
Beirut, 166	Emmaus, 17	Shechem, 38
Bethel, 13	Haifa, 96	Shiloh, 25
Bethlehem, 6	Hebron, 20	Sidon, 163
Bethsaida, 113	Jericho, 20	Scythopolis, 74
Caesarea, 83	Magdala, 103	Tel Aviv, 40
Caesarea Philippi, 138	Megiddo, 72	Tiberias, 98
Cairo, 260	Nain, 78	Tyre, 138

Period 8

CHRIST'S PEREAN MINISTRY

(From after the Feast of the Dedication to Christ's Arrival in Bethany Before the Passover)

January, 30 A.D. to April, 30 A.D.

Matthew 19:1-20:34	Luke 13:23-19:28
Mark 10:1-52	John 10:38-12:1

Jesus Went Across the Jordan into Peraea
Jesus Taught Concerning Humility to the Pharisees
The Second Great Day of Parables
Jesus Raised Lazarus From the Dead
Jesus Went to the City of Ephraim
Jesus Prophesied of His Coming in Glory
Jesus Returned to Peraea
Jesus Answered Questions About Divorce and Eternal Life
Jesus Healed Blind Bartimaeus
Jesus Called Zacchaeus Down From a Tree

248. Jesus went beyond Jordan to where John at first baptized; many came and believed on him there (Jn. 10:39-42). *Unknown location east of the Jordan River, Peraea; January, 30 A.D.*

Note: The Jordan River and Valley—This river, the only large flowing body of water in Palestine, originates in the foothills of Mt. Hermon. After it leaves the Sea of Galilee, it descends to the Dead Sea. The river fertilizes little land beyond its immediate banks, but they are covered with dense vegetation. The river rarely exceeds 100 feet in width, but it overflows its banks in March and April, and becomes as much as a mile wide in the area near Jericho. The river's depth varies between three and twelve feet. The valley is generally less than four miles wide, but it reaches a width of seven miles at Bethshean and fourteen miles at Jericho.

249. Jesus answered the question about how many will be saved: "Strive to enter in at the strait gate: for many, I say unto you, will seek to enter in, and shall not be able" **(Lk. 13:23-30).** *Peraea; Winter, 30 A.D.* ★

250. A pharisee warned Jesus to leave or Herod (Antipas) would kill him. Jesus mourned for Jerusalem and said, "It cannot be that a prophet perish out of Jerusalem" **(Lk. 13:31-35).** *Peraea; the same day, Winter, 30 A.D.*

Note: Peraea—This name does not appear in the Bible, but it refers to the area east of the Jordan River. (This area is known in the gospels as "beyond Jordan.") In Jesus' day it was governed by Herod Antipas. It was less thickly populated than Galilee. The mountains just east of the Jordan Valley form the western border of a broad plateau.

251. Jesus ate in the home of one of the chief Pharisees on the Sabbath day. He healed a man with dropsy, then spoke to the Pharisees about humility: "For whosoever exalteth himself shall be abased; and he that humbleth himself shall be exalted." *Parable:* The Marriage Supper **(Lk. 14:1-24).** *Peraea; Winter, 30 A.D. [★ — Major Discourse #17, Lk. 14:3-24]*

252. Jesus taught the multitude in a second great day of parables (Lk. 14:25-17:10). *Parables:*
    A. Counting the Cost of Building a Tower (14:28-32)
    B. The Lost Sheep (15:4-7) [Compare Mt. 18:12-14]
    C. The Lost Coin (15:8-10)
    D. The Prodigal Son (15:11-32)
    E. The Unjust Steward (16:1-8)
    F. The Rich Man and Lazarus (16:19-31)
Peraea; the same day, Winter, 30 A.D. [★ —Major Discourse #18]

253. Mary and Martha sent word to Jesus that their brother, Lazarus, was sick (Jn. 11:1-5). *Messenger: Bethany to Peraea; Winter, 30 A.D.*

254. Jesus waited two days, then came with his disciples into Judea to Bethany. Lazarus had been dead four days when they arrived (Jn. 11:6-17). *Peraea to Bethany; Winter, 30 A.D.*

255. Jesus comforted Martha and Mary outside of town: "I am the resurrection and the life; he that believeth in me, though he were dead, yet shall he live: And whosoever liveth and believeth in me shall never die" **(Jn. 11:18-37).** *Outside of Bethany; the same day, Winter, 30 A.D.* ★

256. Jesus came to Lazarus' tomb. The stone was rolled away. Jesus called to Lazarus to come forth from the tomb, and he arose from the dead (Jn. 11:38-45). *Lazarus' tomb at Bethany; the same day, Winter, 30 A.D.*

257. Witnesses told the Pharisees of the raising of Lazarus. The chief priests and Pharisees called a council. Caiaphas, the high priest, prophesied that Jesus would die for the nation. They began to plot how to put him to death (Jn. 11:46-53). *Jerusalem; Winter, 30 A.D.*

258. Jesus went with his disciples to the city of Ephraim, and no more walked openly among the Jews (Jn. 11:54). *Bethany to Ephraim; Feb., 30 A.D.*

259. Jesus began his final journey to Jerusalem (Lk. 17:11). *The route: Through Samaria, Galilee, across the Jordan to Peraea, then back across the Jordan through Jericho to Jerusalem; Feb. - early Apr., 30 A.D.*

260. Jesus healed ten lepers and sent them to show themselves unto the priests. Only one, a Samaritan, returned and thanked him. Jesus said: "Were there not ten cleansed? but where are the nine?" **(Lk. 17:12-19).** *An unidentified village, Galilee; Feb.-Mar., 30 A.D.*

261. When the Pharisees asked when the kingdom of God should come, Jesus replied: "The kingdom of God is within you" **(Lk. 17:20-21).** *An unidentified village, Galilee; the same day(?), Feb.-Mar., 30 A.D.* **[★ —Major Discourse #19, Lk. 17:20-18:30]**

262. Jesus prophesied of his coming in glory to his disciples: "For as the lightning, that lighteneth out of one part under heaven, shineth unto the other part under heaven; so shall also the Son of man be in his day" **(Lk. 17:22-37).** *An unidentified village, Galilee; the same day, Feb.-Mar., 30 A.D.* ★

263. Jesus told the parable of the Importunate Widow (Lk. 18: 1-8). *An unidentified village, Galilee; the same day, Feb. - Mar., 30 A.D.* ★

264. Jesus told the parable of the Pharisee and the Publican (Lk. 18:9-14). *An unidentified village, Galilee; the same day, Feb.-Mar., 30 A.D.* ★

265. Jesus left Galilee and came into Peraea (the coasts of Judea beyond Jordan). Multitudes followed him and he taught them there (Mt. 19:1-2; Mk. 10:1). *Galilee to Peraea; Mar., 30 A.D.*

266. Jesus answered the Pharisees' question about divorce: "What therefore God hath joined together, let not man put asunder" **(Mt. 19:3-9; Mk. 10:2-9).** *Peraea; Mar., 30 A.D.* ★

267. Jesus taught more concerning divorce and infidelity to his disciples: "Whosoever shall put away his wife, and marry another, committeth adultery against her" **(Mt. 19:10-12; Mk. 10:10-12).** *In a house, Peraea; the same day(?), Mar., 30 A.D.* ★

268. When little children were brought to Jesus, his disciples rebuked those that brought them, but Jesus said, "Suffer the little children to come unto me, and forbid them not: for of such is the kingdom of God" **(Mk. 10:13-16; Mt. 19:13-15; Lk. 18:15-17).** *Peraea; the same day(?), Mar., 30 A.D.* ★

269. A ruler asked Jesus what he must do to inherit eternal life. Jesus told him to keep the commandments, and then added,

"If thou wilt be perfect, go and sell that thou hast, and give to the poor, and thou shalt have treasure in heaven: and come and follow me" **(Mk. 10:17-22; Mt. 19:16-22; Lk. 18:18-23).** *En route to Jerusalem, Peraea; Mar., 30 A.D.* ★

270. Jesus told his disciples that it is difficult for the rich to enter the kingdom of heaven: "It is easier for a camel to go through the eye of a needle, than for a rich man to enter into the kingdom of God" **(Mk. 10:23-27; Mt. 19:23-26; Lk. 18:24-27).** *En route to Jerusalem, Peraea; the same day, Mar., 30 A.D.* ★

271. Jesus promised the twelve great blessings at the last day: "Ye also shall sit upon twelve thrones, judging the twelve tribes of Israel" **(Mt. 19:27-30; Mk. 10:28-31; Lk. 18:28-30).** *En route to Jerusalem, Peraea; the same day, Mar., 30 A.D.* ★

272. Jesus told the parable of the Laborers in the Vineyard (Mt. 20:1-16). *En route to Jerusalem, Peraea; the same day, Mar., 30 A.D.*

273. Jesus told the Twelve that when they reached Jerusalem he would be betrayed, condemned, mocked, scourged, and crucified, and that on the third day he would rise again (Mk. 10:32-34; Mt. 20:17-19; Lk. 18:31-34). *En route to Jerusalem, Peraea; the same day, Mar., 30 A.D.*

274. James and John and their mother requested that they might sit beside Jesus in his kingdom. Jesus taught the Twelve: "Whosoever will be chief among you, let him be your servant" **(Mk. 10:35-45; Mt. 20:20-28).** *En route to Jerusalem, near Jericho(?); Mar., 30 A.D.*

275. Blind Bartimaeus cried out for Jesus to have mercy on him as the group came to Jericho. Jesus told him: "Receive thy sight: thy faith hath saved thee" **(Mk. 10:46-52; Lk. 18:35-43; Mt. 20:29-34).** *Near Jericho; Mar., 30 A.D.*

276. Zacchaeus, a rich publican from Jericho, climbed a tree so he could see Jesus as he passed through Jericho. Jesus called for him to come down, and went to stay at his house. *Parable:* The Ten Pounds **(Lk. 19:1-27).** [Compare Mt. 25:14-30] *Jericho; Mar., 30 A.D.* ★

277. Jesus ascended up to Jerusalem (Lk. 19:28). *Jericho to Jerusalem; early Apr., 30 A.D.*

Note: The Jerusalem-Jericho Road—This route required a tortuous climb through barren country that continued with little relief for almost twenty miles.

278. Those who came early to the Passover feast at Jerusalem sought Jesus, and wondered if he would come (Jn. 11:55-56). *Jerusalem; early Apr., 30 A.D.*

279. The chief priests and the Pharisees issued a commandment that any man knowing where Jesus was must report it to them

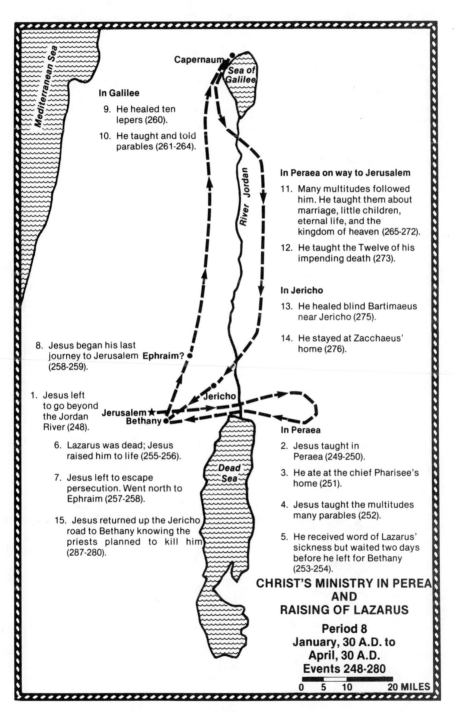

In Galilee

9. He healed ten lepers (260).

10. He taught and told parables (261-264).

In Peraea on way to Jerusalem

11. Many multitudes followed him. He taught them about marriage, little children, eternal life, and the kingdom of heaven (265-272).

12. He taught the Twelve of his impending death (273).

In Jericho

13. He healed blind Bartimaeus near Jericho (275).

14. He stayed at Zacchaeus' home (276).

8. Jesus began his last journey to Jerusalem **Ephraim?** (258-259).

1. Jesus left to go beyond the Jordan River (248).

6. Lazarus was dead; Jesus raised him to life (255-256).

7. Jesus left to escape persecution. Went north to Ephraim (257-258).

15. Jesus returned up the Jericho road to Bethany knowing the priests planned to kill him (287-280).

In Peraea

2. Jesus taught in Peraea (249-250).

3. He ate at the chief Pharisee's home (251).

4. Jesus taught the multitudes many parables (252).

5. He received word of Lazarus' sickness but waited two days before he left for Bethany (253-254).

**CHRIST'S MINISTRY IN PEREA
AND
RAISING OF LAZARUS**

**Period 8
January, 30 A.D. to
April, 30 A.D.
Events 248-280**

0   5   10   20 MILES

so they could take Jesus prisoner (Jn. 11:57). *Jerusalem; early Apr., 30 A.D.*

280. Jesus came to Bethany (Jn. 12:1) *Jericho to Bethany; 6 days before the Passover, Friday or Saturday (Nisan 7 or 8), Apr., 30 A.D.*

Note: **Bethany**—This small city, the home of Mary, Martha and Lazarus, is situated about two miles southeast of Jerusalem on the eastern slope of the Mt. of Olives, on the road from Jericho.

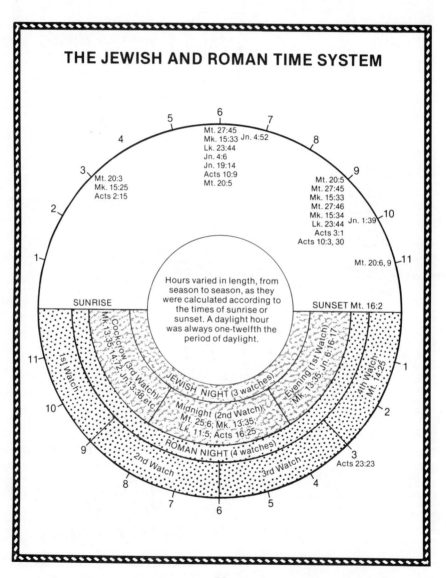

Period 9

CHRIST'S PREPARATION FOR HIS ATONING SACRIFICE

(From Christ's Triumphal Entry into Jerusalem to His Arrest in the Garden of Gethsemane)

Sunday, April 2, 30 A.D. to Thursday, April 6, 30 A.D.

Matthew 21:1-26:56   Luke 19:29-22:53
Mark 11:1-14:52   John 12:12-18:13

Jesus' Triumphal Entry Into Jerusalem
Jesus Cleansed the Temple
Jesus' Third Great Day of Parables
A Voice Answered Jesus from Heaven
Jesus' Great Prophecy of the Last Days
Jesus and the Twelve Ate the Last Supper
Jesus Taught About the Comforter
Jesus Prayed for His Followers
Jesus Suffered in the Garden of Gethsemane
Judas Betrayed Jesus With a Kiss

First Day of the Week—Sunday, April 2

281. When Jesus and his disciples arrived at the Mt. of Olives, nigh unto Bethphage, Jesus sent two disciples to bring an ass and a colt from a nearby village (Mk. 11:1-6; Lk. 19:29-34; Mt. 21:1-6). *Bethany to the Mt. of Olives (about one mile up the southeast slope of the Mt. of Olives); Sunday, April 2, 30 A.D.*

Note: The Mount of Olives—The Mount of Olives is actually a mile-long ridge of hills to the east of the city of Jerusalem, running north and south, curving somewhat around the city from the northeast to the southeast. The Mt. of Olives is not much higher than the city—about 300 feet higher than the temple site, 100 feet above

Zion. It is separated from the city by the Kidron Valley (also known as the Valley of Jehoshaphat). The Mt. of Olives has four independent summits (listed from north to south):

1. "Galilee." This hill is also known as the "Viri Galilaei," and is supposedly the hill where two angels addressed the disciples after Christ's ascension into heaven (Acts 1:11). It is about 400 yards from the "Ascension."

2. "The Ascension" is ¾ of a mile due east of the temple site, and is the actual "Mt. of Olives" of New Testament times. It is believed to be the hill from which Jesus ascended into heaven (Lk. 24:50-53; Acts 1:9-12). The Garden of Gethsemane is at the foot of the hill on the Jerusalem side, and the road to Bethany crosses the summit of the hill.

3. "The Prophets" is the southern spur of "The Ascension." It is subordinate to it and almost a part of it.

4. The "Mount of Offense," ¾ mile southeast of the temple site, is supposed to be the "Mount of Corruption" on which Solomon erected places to worship the strange Gods of his day (1 Ki. 11:7). The road which winds around its southern shoulder is still the most frequented and the best.

Note: **Bethphage**—This area on the eastern slope of the Mt. of Olives, between the summit and Bethany, is the traditional starting point of the Palm Sunday procession. It is not known if there was actually a village by that name. The Talmud indicates that in New Testament times Bethphage was the term for a general area just outside the city walls, which probably extended all around the city. On the east, it extended from the city wall to the base of the Mt. of Olives.

282. The animals were brought; Jesus sat on the colt, and rode into Jerusalem. The multitude spread their garments and palm branches before him and cried: "Hosanna; Blessed is the King of Israel that cometh in the name of the Lord" **(Jn. 12:12-18; Mk. 11:7-10; Lk. 19:35-38; Mt. 21:7-11).** *Crest of the Mt. of Olives to Jerusalem, through the Golden Gate; Sunday, Apr. 2, 30 A.D.*

Note: **The Golden Gate**—Also known as the "Eastern Gate" and "Gate of Mercy," this gate opposite the Mt. of Olives is the only gate that leads directly into the temple area. According to legend, this is to be the spot where the resurrection trumpet will sound and the dead will be raised. Jewish tradition also holds that the Messiah will enter through this gate when he comes to Jerusalem. There is a Moslem cemetery on the east side of the gate. The Turkish governor of Jerusalem had the gate blocked and made into a wall in 1530, in hope of postponing the end of the world and the day of judgment.

283. The Pharisees asked Jesus to rebuke his disciples for their rejoicing. Jesus replied, "If these should hold their peace, the stones would immediately cry out" **(Lk. 19:39-40; Jn. 12:19).** *Approaching Jerusalem; the same day, Sunday, Apr. 2, 30 A.D.*

284. Jesus wept for Jerusalem, and prophesied its destruction (Lk. 19:41-44). *Approaching Jerusalem; the same day, Sunday, Apr. 2, 30 A.D.*

285. Jesus healed the sick and taught in the temple (Mt. 21:14; Lk. 19:47). *Temple of Herod, Jerusalem; the same day, Sunday, Apr. 2, 30 A.D.*

286. The Pharisees objected to Jesus' miracles and the children crying in the temple, but Jesus replied, "Have ye never read, Out of the mouth of babes and sucklings thou hast perfected praise"

(Mt. 21:15-16). *Temple of Herod, Jerusalem; the same day, Sunday, Apr. 2, 30 A.D.*

287. Jesus entered Jerusalem and the temple and observed the activities there (Mk. 11:11). *Temple of Herod and Jerusalem; afternoon of the same day, Sunday, Apr. 2, 30 A.D.*

288. Jesus and his disciples returned to Bethany, and lodged there (Mt. 21:17; Mk. 11:11). *Jerusalem to Bethany; evening of the same day, Sunday, Apr. 2, 30 A.D.*

Second Day of the Week—Monday, April 3

289. Jesus and his disciples returned to Jerusalem (Mk. 11:12; Mt. 21:18). *Bethany to Jerusalem; morning, Monday, Apr. 3, 30 A.D.*

290. Jesus cursed a barren fig tree, and it withered away (Mt. 21:18; Mk. 11:12-14). *En route to Jerusalem; morning, the same day, Monday, Apr. 3, 30 A.D.* ★

291. Jesus again cast out the merchants and moneychangers from the temple: "My house shall be called the house of prayer, but ye have made it a den of thieves" **(Mk. 11:15-17; Mt. 21:12-13; Lk. 19:45-46).** [Compare Jn. 2:14-17] *Temple of Herod, Jerusalem; the same day, Monday, Apr. 3, 30 A.D.*

292. Jesus returned to Bethany (Mk. 11:19). *Jerusalem to Bethany; evening of the same day, Monday, Apr. 3, 30 A.D.*

Third Day of the Week—Tuesday, April 4

293. As Jesus and his disciples came to Jerusalem, they observed the withered fig tree. Jesus commented on faith, prayer and forgiveness: "All things, whatsoever ye shall ask in prayer, believing, ye shall receive" **(Mk. 11:20-26; Mt. 21:20-22).** *Bethany to Jerusalem; morning, Tuesday, Apr. 4, 30 A.D.* ★

294. Jesus was challenged by the chief priests in the temple. When they questioned his authority Jesus countered by asking them about the baptisms performed by John the Baptist (Mt. 21:23-27; Mk. 11:27-33; Lk. 20:1-8). *Temple of Herod; morning, Tuesday, Apr. 4, 30 A.D. [★ —Major Discourse #20, Mt. 21:23-23:39; Mk. 11:27-12:40; Lk. 20:1-47]*

Note: This was Jesus' third "great day of parables."

295. Jesus told the parable of the Two Sons Who Worked in the Vineyard (Mt. 21:28-32). *Temple of Herod; the same day, Tuesday, Apr. 4, 30 A.D.* ★

296. Jesus told the parable of the Wicked Husbandmen (Mt. 21:33-41; Mk. 12:1-9; Lk. 20:9-16). *Temple of Herod; the same day, Tuesday, Apr. 4, 30 A.D.* ★

297. Jesus told the chief priests that the kingdom of God would be taken from them: "The kingdom of God shall be taken from you, and given to a nation bringing forth the fruits thereof" **(Mt. 21:42-44; Lk. 20:17-18; Mk. 12:10-11).** *Temple of Herod; the same day, Tuesday, Apr. 4, 30 A.D.* ★

298. The chief priests and Parisees were afraid to lay hold of Jesus because they feared the multitude, which took Jesus for a prophet. They left. (Mt. 21:45-46; Lk. 20:19; Mk. 12:12). *Temple of Herod; the same day, Tuesday, Apr. 4, 30 A.D.*

299. Jesus told the parable of the Marriage of the King's Son (Mt. 22:1-14). *Temple of Herod; the same day, Tuesday, Apr. 4, 30 A.D.* ★

300. The chief priests left, but sent other Pharisees and Herodians to catch him in his words. When they asked if it was lawful to give tribute to Caesar, Jesus answered, "Render to Caesar the things that are Caesar's, and to God the things that are God's" **(Mt. 22:15-22; Mk. 12:13-17; Lk. 20:20-26).** *Temple of Herod; the same day, Tuesday, Apr. 4, 30 A.D.* ★

301. Jesus answered the Sadducees' question about marriage after the resurrection: "Ye do err, not knowing the scriptures, nor the power of God" **(Mt. 22:23-33; Mk. 12:18-27; Lk. 20:27-40).** *Temple of Herod; the same day, Tuesday, Apr. 4, 30 A.D.*

302. A lawyer asked which is the great commandment in the law. Jesus replied, "Thou shalt love the Lord thy God" **and** "thy neighbor as thyself" **(Mk. 12:28-34; Mt. 22:35-40).** [Compare Lk. 10:25-37] *Temple of Herod; the same day, Tuesday, Apr. 4, 30 A.D.*

303. Jesus asked the Pharisees how the scribes say that Christ is the Son of David: "David therefore himself called him Lord; and whence is he then his son? **(Mt. 22:41-46; Mk. 12:35-37; Lk. 20:41-44).** *Temple of Herod; the same day, Tuesday, Apr. 4, 30 A.D.* ★

304. Jesus denounced the scribes and Pharisees: "Woe unto you, scribes and Pharisees, hypocrites! for ye shut up the kingdom of heaven against men" **(Mt. 23:1-36; Mk. 12:38-40; Lk. 20:45-47).** *Temple of Herod; the same day, Tuesday, Apr. 4, 30 A.D.* ★

305. Jesus lamented over Jerusalem (Mt. 23:37-39). [Compare Lk. 13:34-35] *Temple of Herod; the same day, Tuesday, Apr. 4, 30 A.D.*

306. Jesus observed a widow casting her mites into the treasury: "She of her want did cast in all that she had, even all her living" **(Mk. 12:41-44; Lk. 21:1-4).** *Temple of Herod; the same day, Tuesday, Apr. 4, 30 A.D.*

Note: **Treasury**—According to the Talmud, thirteen chests, marked for various contributions, were kept in the temple's Court of the Women. These were emptied prior to each of the three major feasts (Passover, Pentecost, and Tabernacles).

307. People from Greece who were at the feast sought Jesus in the temple. He told them that the hour had come for the Son of man to be glorified. When Jesus said, Father, glorify thy name, there came a voice from heaven: "I have both glorified it, and will glorify it again" **(Jn. 12:20-36).** [Compare Mt. 3:17; 17:5] *Temple of Herod; afternoon of the same day, Tuesday, Apr. 4, 30 A.D.* **[★ —Major Discourse #21]**

308. Jesus departed and hid himself from them (Jn. 12:36). *Temple of Herod; afternoon of the same day, Tuesday, Apr. 4, 30 A.D.*

Note: Public Ministry Closed—This event, and Jesus' subsequent departure, marked the end of his public ministry. From this point on in the gospels, Jesus' comments were reserved for his intimate disciples only.

309. Many didn't believe on Jesus. Some of the chief rulers did, but did not confess him, "For they loved the praise of men more than the praise of God" **(Jn. 12:37-43).** *Jerusalem; Tuesday, Apr. 4, 30 A.D.*

310. Jesus spoke of his relationship with his Father: "I have not spoken of myself; but the Father which sent me, he gave me a commandment, what I should say, and what I should speak" **(Jn. 12:44-50).** *Jerusalem; Tuesday, Apr. 4, 30 A.D.* ★

311. Jesus departed from the temple, and prophesied, "There shall not be left here one stone upon another, that shall not be thrown down" **(Mt. 24:1-2; Mk. 13:1-2; Lk. 21:5-6).** *Leaving the temple of Herod; afternoon of the same day, Tuesday, Apr. 4, 30 A.D.* ★

312. Jesus went out to the Mt. of Olives. When his disciples asked when Jerusalem would be destroyed and when the end of the world would come, Jesus gave his great Olivet discourse (Mt. 24:3-51; Mk. 13:3-37; Lk. 21:7-36). *Mt. of Olives; afternoon of the same day, Tuesday, Apr. 4, 30 A.D.* **[★ —Major Discourse #22, Mt. 24:3-25:46; Mk. 13:3-37; Lk. 21:7-36]**

313. Jesus told the parable of the Ten Virgins (Mt. 25:1-13). *Mt. of Olives; afternoon of the same day, Tuesday, Apr. 4, 30 A.D.* ★

314. Jesus told the parable of the Talents (Mt. 25:14-30). [Compare Lk. 19:12-27] *Mt. of Olives; afternoon of the same day, Tuesday, Apr. 4, 30 A.D.* ★

315. Jesus prophesied of the final judgment: "Before him shall be gathered all nations: and he shall separate them one from another, as a shepherd divideth his sheep from the goats" **(Mt. 25:31-33).** *Mt. of Olives; afternoon of the same day, Tuesday, Apr. 4, 30 A.D.* ★

316. Jesus spoke of service as a criterion for the judgment: "Inasmuch as ye have done it unto one of the least of these my brethren, ye have done it unto me" **(Mt. 25:34-46).** *Mt. of Olives; afternoon of the same day, Tuesday, Apr. 4, 30 A.D.* ★

317. Jesus foretold his death: "After two days is the feast of the passover, and the Son of man is betrayed to be crucified" **(Mt. 26:1-2).** *Mt. of Olives; afternoon of the same day, Tuesday, Apr. 4, 30 A.D.*

318. The chief priests met in Caiaphas' palace and plotted to kill Jesus (Mt. 26:3-5; Mk. 14:1-2; Lk. 22:1-2). *Caiaphas' palace, Jerusalem; Tuesday, Apr. 4, 30 A.D.*

319. Jesus returned to Bethany (Mt. 26:6; Mk. 14:3). *Jerusalem to Bethany; evening of the same day, Tuesday, Apr. 4, 30 A.D.*

320. Mary anointed Jesus at Simon's supper. When Judas Iscariot complained, Jesus said, "Against the day of my burying hath she kept this. For the poor always ye have with you; but me ye have not always" **(Jn. 12:2-9; Mt. 26:6-13; Mk. 14:3-9).** [Compare Lk. 7:36-50] *Home of Simon the leper (a near relation of Lazarus?); night of the same day, Tuesday, Apr. 4, 30 A.D.*

Fourth Day of the Week—Wednesday, April 5

321. Christ taught in the temple, and at night abode in the Mt. of Olives (Lk. 21:37-38).

Note: **Wednesday Activities**—The chronological application of these verses is uncertain. Many commentators show Jesus "in retirement at Bethany" on this day; some place the suppper at the home of Simon the leper on this night. "Abode in the mount of Olives" can easily mean Bethany, which was located on the eastern slope of the ridge.

322. Judas Iscariot went to the chief priests and covenanted to betray Jesus for thirty pieces of silver (Mt. 26:14-16; Lk. 22:3-6; Mk. 14:10-11). *Jerusalem; Judas went from Bethany to Jerusalem to Bethany(?); day uncertain, Apr., 30 A.D.*

Fifth Day of the Week—Thursday, April 6

323. Jesus sent Peter and John to arrange for a room in Jerusalem where they could eat together (Lk. 22:7-13; Mk. 14:12-16; Mt. 26:17-19). *Bethany to Jerusalem, to a house with an upper room; Thursday afternoon, Apr. 6, 30 A.D.*

324. Jesus and the Twelve came to the upper room and sat down to eat (Mt. 26:20; Mk. 14:17-18; Lk. 22:14). *The upper room, Jerusalem; evening of the same day, Apr. 6, 30 A.D.*

325. They ate the passover meal. Jesus said, "I will not any more eat thereof, until it be fulfilled in the kingdom of God" **(Lk. 22:15-18).** *The upper room, Jerusalem; evening of the same day, Thursday, Apr. 6, 30 A.D.*

326. Jesus instituted the sacrament of the Lord's supper, with the bread and cup: "This is my blood of the new testament, which is shed for many for the remission of sins" **(Mt. 26:26-29; Mk. 14:22-25; Lk. 22:19-20).** *The upper room, Jerusalem; the same night, Thursday, Apr. 6, 30 A.D.* ★

327. Jesus washed the feet of his disciples: "He that is washed needeth not save to wash his feet, but is clean every whit: and ye are clean . . ." **(Jn. 13:2-15).** *The upper room, Jerusalem; night, the same night, Thursday, Apr. 6, 30 A.D.* ★

328. Jesus told his disciples to serve one another: "He that is greatest among you, let him be as the younger; and he that is chief, as he that doth serve" **(Lk. 22:24-30; Jn. 13:13-17).** [Compare Mk. 9:33-37; Mt. 23:10-12] *The upper room, Jerusalem; the same night, Thursday, Apr. 6, 30 A.D.* ★

329. Jesus told the Twelve that he would be betrayed, and privately indicated that Judas would betray him: "He that dippeth his hand with me in the dish, the same shall betray me" **(Mt. 26:21-25; Mk. 14:18-21; Lk. 22:21-23; Jn. 13:18-26).** *The upper room, Jerusalem; the same night, Thursday, Apr. 6, 30 A.D.* ★

330. Jesus told Judas, "That thou doest, do quickly," **Judas left immediately (Jn. 13:27-30).** *The upper room, Jerusalem, the same night, Thursday, Apr. 6, 30 A.D.*

331. Peter declared his loyalty to Jesus, but Jesus warned that he would deny him: "The cock shall not crow, till thou hast denied me thrice" **(Lk. 22:31-34; Jn. 13:36-38).** *The upper room, Jerusalem; the same night, Thursday, Apr. 6, 30 A.D.*

332. Jesus taught the Twelve about the Comforter: "The Holy Ghost, whom the Father will send in my name, he shall teach you all things, and bring all things to your remembrance" **(Jn. 14:1-16:33).** *Parable:* The True Vine. *The upper room, Jerusalem; the same night, Thursday, Apr. 6, 30 A.D. [★ —Major Discourse #23]*

333. Jesus prayed for his followers: "Neither pray I for these alone, but for them also which shall believe on me through their word; That they all may be one" **(Jn. 17:1-26).** *The upper room, Jerusalem; the same night, Thursday, Apr. 6, 30 A.D. [★ —Major Discourse #24]*

334. They sang a hymn, and went out to the Mt. of Olives (Mt. 26:30; Mk. 14:26; Lk. 22:39). *To the Mt. of Olives; the same night, Thursday, Apr. 6, 30 A.D.*

335. The disciples pledged their loyalty when Jesus told them, "All ye shall be offended because of me this night" **(Mt. 26:31-35; Mk. 14:27-31).** *En route to the Mt. of Olives; the same night, Thursday, Apr. 6, 30 A.D.*

336. Jesus and his disciples came to Gethsemane. Jesus instructed his disciples to wait there while he took Peter, James and John farther into the garden to pray (Mt. 26:36-37; Mk. 14:32-33; Jn. 18:1). *The Garden of Gethsemane, on the Mt. of Olives; the same night, Thursday, Apr. 6, 30 A.D.*

337. Jesus told Peter, James and John to watch and pray while he prayed alone. An angel appeared and strengthened him. His

75

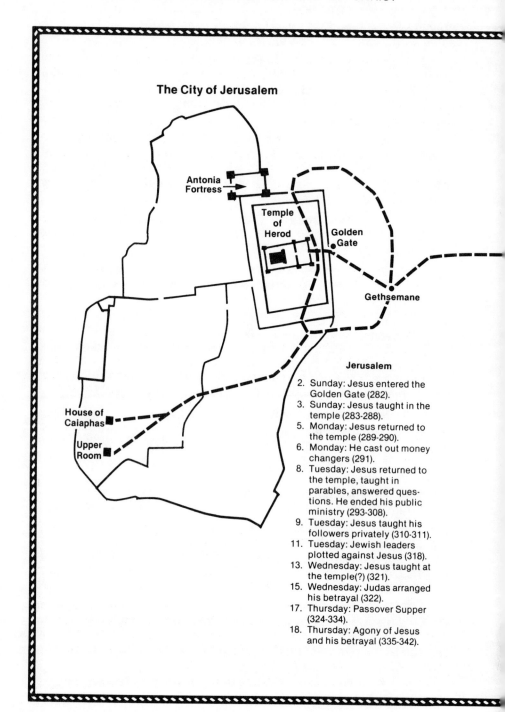

The City of Jerusalem

Antonia Fortress

Temple of Herod

Golden Gate

Gethsemane

House of Caiaphas

Upper Room

Jerusalem

2. Sunday: Jesus entered the Golden Gate (282).
3. Sunday: Jesus taught in the temple (283-288).
5. Monday: Jesus returned to the temple (289-290).
6. Monday: He cast out money changers (291).
8. Tuesday: Jesus returned to the temple, taught in parables, answered questions. He ended his public ministry (293-308).
9. Tuesday: Jesus taught his followers privately (310-311).
11. Tuesday: Jewish leaders plotted against Jesus (318).
13. Wednesday: Jesus taught at the temple(?) (321).
15. Wednesday: Judas arranged his betrayal (322).
17. Thursday: Passover Supper (324-334).
18. Thursday: Agony of Jesus and his betrayal (335-342).

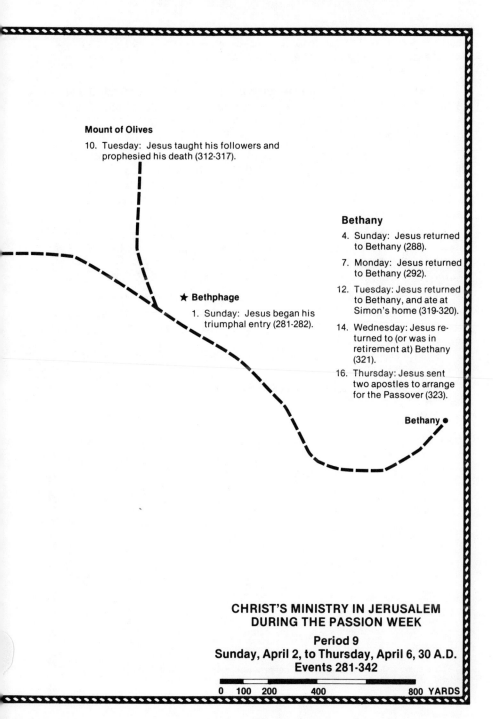

Mount of Olives

10. Tuesday: Jesus taught his followers and prophesied his death (312-317).

Bethany

4. Sunday: Jesus returned to Bethany (288).

7. Monday: Jesus returned to Bethany (292).

12. Tuesday: Jesus returned to Bethany, and ate at Simon's home (319-320).

14. Wednesday: Jesus returned to (or was in retirement at) Bethany (321).

16. Thursday: Jesus sent two apostles to arrange for the Passover (323).

★ **Bethphage**

1. Sunday: Jesus began his triumphal entry (281-282).

Bethany ●

CHRIST'S MINISTRY IN JERUSALEM DURING THE PASSION WEEK

Period 9
Sunday, April 2, to Thursday, April 6, 30 A.D.
Events 281-342

0   100   200   400   800 YARDS

sweat was as great drops of blood. He returned three times and each time found them asleep (Lk. 22:40-46; Mt. 26:38-46; Mk. 14:34-42). *The Garden of Gethsemane, on the Mt. of Olives; the same night, Thursday, Apr. 6, 30 A.D.* ★

338. Judas Iscariot came with a multitude and betrayed Jesus with a kiss. The guards seized Jesus (Jn. 18:2-9; Mt. 26:47-50; Mk. 14:43-46; Lk. 22:47-48). *The Garden of Gethsemane, on the Mt. of Olives; the same night, Thursday, Apr. 6, 30 A.D.*

339. Peter drew his sword, and cut off the right ear of Malchus, the high priest's servant. Jesus told Peter to put up his sword, then touched the ear and healed it (Jn. 18:10-11; Mt. 26:51-54; Lk. 22:50-51; Mk. 14:47). *The Garden of Gethsemane, on the Mt. of Olives; the same night, Thursday, Apr. 6, 30 A.D.* ★

340. Jesus rebuked the multitude for capturing him by stealth: "I sat daily with you teaching in the temple, and ye laid no hold on me" **(Mt. 26:55-56; Mk. 14:48-49; Lk. 22:52-54).** *The Garden of Gethsemane, on the Mt. of Olives; the same night, Thursday, Apr. 6, 30 A.D.*

341. All of the disciples forsook Jesus, and fled; one young man lost his linen cloth and fled naked (Mk. 14:50-52; Mt. 26:56). *The Garden of Gethsemane, on the Mt. of Olives; the same night, Thursday, Apr. 6, 30 A.D.*

Note: Mark—Many commentators think this young man was Mark, author of the gospel which records the incident.

342. Jesus was bound and led away (Jn. 18:12-13). *From the Garden of Gethsemane back to Jerusalem; the same night, Thursday, Apr. 6, 30 A.D.*

MONEY IN NEW TESTAMENT TIMES
(extremely simplified)

Relative Value	Jewish	Greek	Roman
1	1 lepton, or mite		½ quadrans
2	1 farthing		1 quadrans
8	4 farthings		1 as or assarion
128		1 drachma	1 denarius or "penny"
512		1 stater	4 denarii
3,200		25 drachmai	1 aureus
12,000	60 shekels	1 mina	100 denarii or "pounds"
768,000	1 talent	1 talent	240 aurei

Some items listed above were coins, others were units of weight measurement. Gold held 13.5 times the value of silver. One Roman penney represented a good day's wage.

Period 10

CHRIST'S TRIAL, CRUCIFIXION AND BURIAL

(From Christ's Appearance Before Annas to His Burial)

Early Friday Morning, April 7, 30 A.D. to Early Sunday Morning, April 9, 30 A.D.

Matthew 26:57-17:66   Luke 22:54-23:56
Mark 14:53-15:47   John 18:13-19:42

Jesus Was Taken to Annas
Jesus Was Judged Guilty of Death by Caiaphas
Peter Thrice Betrayed the Savior
The Sanhedrin Formalized the Verdict
Jesus Was Taken to Herod
Pilate Sent Jesus to Herod Antipas
Pilate Sentenced Jesus to Death
Jesus Was Crucified and Buried

Sixth Day of the Week—April 7 (Good Friday)

343. Jesus was taken, bound, to Annas, the former high priest and father-in-law of Caiaphas the high priest (Jn. 18:13-14). *House of Annas, Jerusalem; very early Friday morning before sunrise, Apr. 7, 30 A.D.*

344. Annas sent Jesus, bound, to the palace of Caiaphas, the high priest. John(?) went in with Jesus, while Peter remained outside (Mk. 14:53-54; Mt. 26:57-58; Lk. 22:54; Jn. 18:24). *Caiaphas' palace, Jerusalem; very early Friday morning before sunrise, Apr. 7, 30 A.D.*

345. The high priest, with the chief priests, elders, and scribes, asked Jesus of his disciples, and of his doctrine. When a guard

struck Jesus in the face, Jesus answered him, "If I have spoken evil, bear witness of the evil: but if well, why smitest thou me?" **(Jn. 18:19-23).** *Caiaphas' palace, Jerusalem; very early Friday morning before sunrise, Apr. 7, 30 A.D.*

346. False witnesses spoke against Jesus, but their testimonies didn't agree. When Jesus acknowledged to Caiaphas that he was truly the Son of God, Caiaphas accused him of blasphemy and the informal gathering agreed he was guilty of death (Mk. 14:55-64; Mt. 26:59-66). *Caiaphas' palace, Jerusalem; very early Friday morning before sunrise, Apr. 7, 30 A.D.*

347. The Jewish guards blindfolded and mocked Jesus. They struck him and spoke blasphemies to him (Lk. 22:63-65; Mt. 26:67-68; Mk. 14:65). *Caiaphas' palace, Jerusalem; early Friday morning, Apr. 7, 30 A.D.*

348. Peter, waiting outside Caiaphas' palace, three times denied that he was one of Jesus' disciples, and immediately the cock crew (Mt. 26:69-75; Mk. 14:66-72; Lk. 22:55-62; Jn. 18:25-27). *Outside Caiaphas' palace, Jerusalem; at sunrise, Friday, Apr. 7, 30 A.D.*

349. The Sanhedrin held a formal meeting at dawn and formalized their verdict against Jesus reached in their previous meeting (Mt. 27:1; Mk. 15:1; Lk. 22:66-71). *Caiaphas' palace, Jerusalem; dawn Friday morning, Apr. 7, 30 A.D.*

350. The multitude took Jesus to the hall of judgment where Pontius Pilate, the Roman Procurator (provincial governor), was staying (Mt. 27:2; Mk. 15:1; Lk. 23:1; Jn. 18:28). *Roman hall of judgment, probably part of the Fortress of Antonia; morning, the same day, Friday, Apr. 7, 30 A.D.*

351. Judas Iscariot returned the 30 pieces of silver to the chief priests in the temple, then went and hanged himself (Mt. 27:3-10). [Compare Acts 1:18] *Temple of Herod, Jerusalem; the same day, Friday, Apr. 7, 30 A.D.*

352. Jesus was tried by Pilate, who found no fault in him. When Pilate asked "Art thou the King of the Jews?" **Jesus answered,** "My kingdom is not of this world: if my kingdom were of this world, then would my servants fight, that I should not be delivered to the Jews" **(Jn. 18:28-38; Mt. 27:11-14; Mk. 15:2-5; Lk. 23:2-5).** *Fortress of Antonia, Jerusalem; morning of the same day, Friday, Apr. 7, 30 A.D.*

353. Pilate sent Jesus to be tried by Herod Antipas. Jesus refused to answer any questions. Herod's men mocked Jesus, arrayed him in a gorgeous robe, and returned him to Pilate (Lk. 23:7-12). *Herod's palace(?), Jerusalem (Herod Antipas' home and capital was in Tiberias—he was probably in Jerusalem for the passover and staying at the family's palace built by his father, Herod the Great); morning of the same day, Friday, Apr. 7, 30 A.D.*

354. Pilate told the Jews he found no fault in Jesus worthy of death, and announced he would chastise and release him. The Jews clamored for Barabbas to be released and for Jesus to be crucified (Mt. 27:15-18, 20-23; Mk. 15:6-14; Lk. 23:13-23; Jn. 18:39-40). *Fortress of Antonia, Jerusalem; morning of the same day, Friday, Apr. 7, 30 A.D.*

355. Pilate's wife sent a message to Pilate telling him to have nothing to do with Jesus because of a dream she had received (Mt. 27:19). *Fortress of Antonia, Jerusalem; morning of the same day, Friday, Apr. 7, 30 A.D.*

356. Pilate washed his hands as a symbol he was innocent of Christ's blood. The people all answered, "His blood be on us, and on our children" **(Mt. 27:24-25).** *Fortress of Antonia, Jerusalem; morning of the same day, Friday, Apr. 7, 30 A.D.*

357. Pilate sentenced Jesus to death (Lk. 23:24). *Fortress of Antonia, Jerusalem; morning of the same day, Friday, Apr. 7, 30 A.D.*

358. Pilate released Barabbas to the multitude (Mt. 27:26; Mk. 15:15; Lk. 23:25). *Fortress of Antonia, Jerusalem; morning of the same day, Friday, Apr. 7, 30 A.D.*

359. Jesus was scourged (Mt. 27:26; Mk. 15:15; Jn. 19:1). *Fortress of Antonia, Jerusalem; morning of the same day, Friday, Apr. 7, 30 A.D.*

360. The Roman soldiers took Jesus to the Praetorium (common hall), where they made him a crown of thorns, put a scarlet robe on him, and mocked him (Mt. 27:27-30; Mk. 15:16-19; Jn. 19:2-3). *Fortress of Antonia, Jerusalem; morning of the same day, Friday, Apr. 7, 30 A.D.*

361. Pilate brought Jesus out to the crowd once again, and told them "I find no fault in him" **(Jn. 19:4-7).** *Fortress of Antonia, Jerusalem; morning of the same day, Friday, Apr. 7, 30 A.D.*

362. Pilate again questioned Jesus, who said, "Thou couldest have no power at all against me, except it were given thee from above" **(Jn. 19:8-12).** *Fortress of Antonia, Jerusalem; morning of the same day, Friday, Apr. 7, 30 A.D.*

363. Pilate sat in the judgment seat and said "Behold your king!" **when the chief priests answered** "We have no king but Caesar," **Pilate delivered Jesus to be crucified (Jn. 19:13-16).** *Fortress of Antonia, Jerusalem; the sixth hour (about noon), the same day, Friday, Apr. 7, 30 A.D.*

364. They put Jesus' rainment on him and led him away to crucify him (Mt. 27:31; Mk. 15:20; Jn. 19:16). *Fortress of Antonia, Jerusalem; about noon, the same day, Friday, Apr. 7, 30 A.D.*

365. The soldiers compelled Simon, from Cyrene, to walk behind Jesus and carry his cross (Lk. 23:26; Mt. 27:32; Mk. 15:21).

The way of the cross, Jerusalem; about noon, the same day, Friday, Apr. 7, 30 A.D.

366. A great company of people followed them, mourning. Jesus said to the women, "Daughters of Jerusalem, weep not for me, but weep for yourselves, and for your children" **(Lk. 23:27-31).** *The way of the cross, Jerusalem; about noon, the same day, Friday, Apr. 7, 30 A.D.*

Note: Stations of the Cross—Visitors to Jerusalem usually walk along the Via Dolorosa, which is the road believed to have been followed by the Savior as he moved from the Praetorium to Calvary. The Catholic church has identified fourteen stations along the way with numbers or inscriptions. Some of these stations commemorate events preserved by tradition rather than scripture. The fourteen stations are: (1) Jesus is condemned to death, (2) Jesus receives the cross, (3) Jesus falls the first time, (4) Jesus meets his afflicted mother, (5) Simon of Cyrene helps Jesus to carry his cross, (6) Veronica wipes the face of Jesus, (7) Jesus falls the second time, (8) Jesus speaks to the daughters of Jerusalem, (9) Jesus falls the third time, (10) Jesus is stripped of his garments, (11) Jesus is nailed to the cross, (12) Jesus dies on the cross, (13) The body of Jesus is taken down from the cross, and (14) Jesus is laid in the sepulchre.

367. They came to Calvary, also called Golgotha, the place of a skull (Lk. 23:33; Mt. 27:33; Mk. 15:22; Jn. 19:17). *Golgotha, outside the Jerusalem wall (to the west, opposite the Fortress of Antonia); about noon, the same day, Friday, Apr. 7, 30 A.D.*

368. They gave Jesus vinegar mingled with gall to drink, but Jesus refused it (Mt. 27:34; Mk. 15:23). *Golgotha, outside Jerusalem; about noon, the same day, Friday, Apr. 7, 30 A.D.*

369. Jesus was crucified: nailed to the cross. Two thieves were also hung on crosses, one on each side of him (Lk. 23:32-33; Mt. 27:35, 38; Mk. 15:24-25, 27-28; Jn. 19:18). *Golgotha, outside Jerusalem; about noon, the same day, Friday, Apr. 7, 30 A.D.*

Note: Verse 25, "the third hour" (9 a.m.) is at variance with Jn. 19:14, "the sixth hour" (12 noon). The hour was probably in between the two times.

370. Pilate wrote a title in Hebrew, Greek and Latin, and put it on the cross: "Jesus of Nazareth the King of the Jews" **(Jn. 19:19-22; Mt. 27:37; Mk. 15:26; Lk. 23:37-38).** *Golgotha, outside Jerusalem; about noon, the same day, Friday, Apr. 7, 30 A.D.*

371. The soldiers cast lots and divided his garments among them, and then sat down to watch (Jn. 19:23-24; Mt. 27:35-36; Mk. 15:24; Lk. 23:34). *Golgotha, outside Jerusalem; about noon, the same day, Friday, Apr. 7, 30 A.D.*

372. Jesus' first words from the cross: "Father, forgive them; for they know not what they do" **(Lk. 23:34).** *Golgotha, outside Jerusalem; early afternoon, the same day, Friday, Apr. 7, 30 A.D.*

373. The multitude, chief priests, soldiers, and the thieves mocked Jesus (Mt. 27:39-44; Mk. 15:29-32; Lk. 23:35-37). *Golgotha, outside Jerusalem; early afternoon, the same day, Friday, Apr. 7, 30 A.D.*

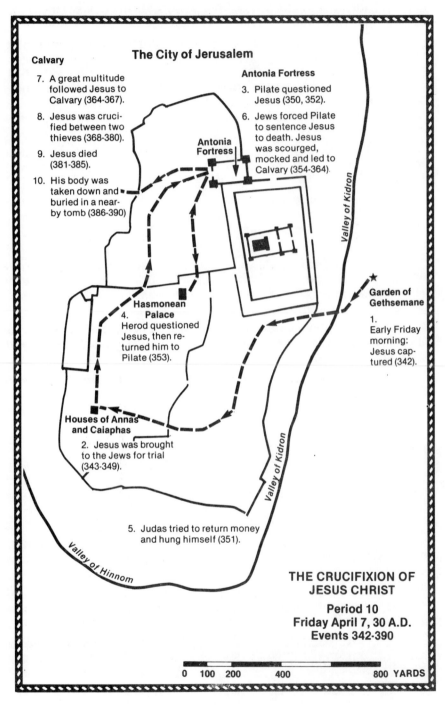

The City of Jerusalem

Calvary

7. A great multitude followed Jesus to Calvary (364-367).

8. Jesus was crucified between two thieves (368-380).

9. Jesus died (381-385).

10. His body was taken down and buried in a nearby tomb (386-390)

Antonia Fortress

3. Pilate questioned Jesus (350, 352).

6. Jews forced Pilate to sentence Jesus to death. Jesus was scourged, mocked and led to Calvary (354-364).

Antonia Fortress

Hasmonean Palace

4. Herod questioned Jesus, then returned him to Pilate (353).

Garden of Gethsemane

1. Early Friday morning: Jesus captured (342).

Houses of Annas and Caiaphas

2. Jesus was brought to the Jews for trial (343-349).

5. Judas tried to return money and hung himself (351).

Valley of Kidron

Valley of Kidron

Valley of Hinnom

THE CRUCIFIXION OF JESUS CHRIST

Period 10
Friday April 7, 30 A.D.
Events 342-390

0   100   200   400   800   YARDS

374. Jesus' second words from the cross, in answer to one of the thieve's request for Jesus to remember him in his kingdom: "Verily I say unto thee, To day shalt thou be with me in paradise" **(Lk. 23:39-43).** *Golgotha, outside Jerusalem; early afternoon, the same day, Friday, Apr. 7, 30 A.D.*

375. Jesus' third words from the cross, to his mother and to the disciple John: "Woman, behold thy son! Behold thy mother!" **(Jn. 19:25-27).** *Golgotha, outside Jerusalem; early afternoon, the same day, Friday, Apr. 7, 30 A.D.*

376. There was darkness over all the earth from the sixth to the ninth hour (Lk. 23:44-45; Mt. 27:45; Mk. 15:33). *Over all the land; from noon to 3 p.m., the same day, Friday, Apr. 7, 30 A.D.*

377. Jesus' fourth words from the cross: "My God, my God, why hast thou forsaken me?" **(Mt. 27:46-47; Mk. 15:34-35).** *Golgotha, outside Jerusalem; about the ninth hour (3 p.m.), the same day, Friday, Apr. 7, 30 A.D.*

378. Jesus' fifth words from the cross: "I thirst." **They filled a sponge with vinegar, and gave it to him to drink (Jn. 19:28-29; Mt. 27:48-49; Mk. 15:36).** *Golgotha, outside Jerusalem; about the ninth hour (3 p.m.), the same day, Friday, Apr. 7, 30 A.D.*

379. Jesus' sixth words from the cross: "It is finished" **(Jn. 19:30).** *Golgotha, outside Jerusalem; about the ninth hour (3 p.m.), the same day, Friday, Apr. 7, 30 A.D.*

380. Jesus' seventh words from the cross: "Father, into thy hands I commend my spirit" **(Lk. 23:46).** *Golgotha, outside Jerusalem; about the ninth hour (3 p.m.), the same day, Friday, Apr. 7, 30 A.D.*

381. Jesus bowed his head, and gave up the ghost (Jn. 19:30; Mt. 27:50; Mk. 15:37; Lk. 23:46). *Golgotha, outside Jerusalem; about the ninth hour (3 p.m.), the same day, Friday, Apr. 7, 30 A.D.*

382. The veil of the temple was rent in the midst (Mt. 27:51; Mk. 15:38; Lk. 23:45). *Temple of Herod, Jerusalem; afternoon, the same day, Friday, Apr. 7, 30 A.D.*

383. The soldiers watching Jesus were frightened; the centurion exclaimed, "Truly this was the Son of God" **(Mt. 27:54; Mk. 15:39; Lk. 23:47).** *Golgotha, outside Jerusalem; about the ninth hour (3 p.m.), the same day, Friday, Apr. 7, 30 A.D.*

384. There were many women followers of Jesus from Galilee standing far off watching, including Mary Magdalene, Mary the mother of James and Joses; and Salome, the mother of Zebedee's children (Mt. 27:55-56; Mk. 15:40-41; Lk. 23:49). *Near Golgotha, outside Jerusalem; about the ninth hour (3 p.m.), the same day, Friday, Apr. 7, 30 A.D.*

385. The Jews requested of Pilate that the three be killed and taken away before the beginning of the Sabbath day. The soldiers broke the legs of the two thieves, pierced Jesus' side (Jn. 19:31-37). *Fortress of Antonia(?), Jerusalem, and Golgotha; late afternoon, the same day, Friday, Apr. 7, 30 A.D.*

386. Joseph of Arimathaea obtained permission from Pilate to take Jesus' body down from the cross (Mk. 15:42-45; Mt. 27:57-58; Lk. 23:50-52; Jn. 19:38). *Fortress of Antonia(?), Jerusalem; late afternoon, the same day, Friday, Apr. 7, 30 A.D.*

387. Joseph of Arimathaea and Nicodemus took the body of Jesus and prepared it for burial (Jn. 19:38-40; Mt. 27:59; Mk. 15:46; Lk. 23:53). *Garden near Golgotha(?); early evening, the same day, Friday, Apr. 7, 30 A.D.*

388. Jesus' body was buried in a new sepulchre, which belonged to Joseph of Arimathaea, in a garden near Golgotha. A stone was rolled in front of the tomb. (Jn. 19:41-42; Mt. 27:60; Mk. 15:46; Lk. 23:53). *Garden tomb near Golgotha, outside Jerusalem; early evening, the same day, Friday, Apr. 7, 30 A.D.*

389. Mary Magdalene and Mary the mother of Joses watched the burial. They returned (to Jerusalem?) and prepared spices and ointments (Lk. 23:55-56; Mt. 27:61; Mk. 15:47). *Garden tomb near Golgotha, outside Jerusalem; early evening, the same day, Friday, Apr. 7, 30 A.D.*

Seventh Day of the Week—Saturday, April 8 (Easter Eve)

390. The chief priests and Pharisees came to Pilate and obtained permission to set a guard on the tomb so Jesus' body wouldn't be stolen. They sealed the tomb and set a watch (Mt. 27:62-66). *Fortress of Antonia(?) and Garden tomb; the next day, Saturday, Apr. 8, 30 A.D.*

DEATH BY CRUCIFIXION

Crucifixion was practiced by the Carthaginians and Phoenicians, and was used extensively by the Romans for executing slaves, provincials, and criminals (but rarely Roman citizens). Three types of cross were used: the St. Anthony's cross (t-shaped), the St. Andrew's cross (x-shaped), and a cross with two crossbeams. After condemnation, victims were scourged, then made to carry their cross outside the city. He was then stripped and laid on the ground with the crossbeam under his shoulders, and his arms or hands tied or nailed to it. The crossbar was then lifted and secured to the upright post so the victim's feet were just clear of the ground, then the feet were tied or nailed. The weight of the body usually rested on a peg, upon which the victim sat. The condemned man was then left to die from exhaustion and the severe pain caused by spasmodic contractions and severe cramps, as well as from his wounds and scourging. Death was sometimes hastened by breaking his legs. Truly the Lord Jesus Christ *suffered* for the transgressions of mankind.

Period 11

CHRIST'S RESURRECTION AND ASCENSION

(From the Opening of Jesus' Tomb Through His Ascension into Heaven)

Sunday, April 9, 30 A.D. to Thursday, May 18, 30 A.D.

Matthew 28:1-20	Luke 24:1-53
Mark 16:1-19	John 20:1-21:25
1 Cor. 15:5-7	Acts 1:1-12

An Earthquake and Angel Opened Jesus' Tomb
Many Saints Were Resurrected and Seen
    in Jerusalem
The Women Saw Angels in the Tomb
Jesus Appeared to Mary Magdalene
The Priests Bribed the Guards to Lie
Jesus Appeared to His Disciples in Emmaus
Jesus Appeared to His Disciples in Jerusalem
Jesus Appeared to His Disciples in Galilee
Jesus Ascended into Heaven

391. A great earthquake occurred at dawn. An angel rolled the stone away from the door, and sat upon it. The guards were afraid, and fainted (Mt. 28:2-4). *Garden tomb, outside Jerusalem; dawn, Sunday, Apr. 9, 30 A.D.*

392. The graves were opened, and many bodies of the saints arose, and came out of the graves after Jesus' resurrection, and went into Jerusalem and appeared to many (Mt. 27:52-53). *Jerusalem; Sunday, Apr. 9, 30 A.D.*

393. Mary Magdalene, Mary the mother of James, the other Mary, Salome, Joanna and other women came to the tomb and found the stone rolled away. (Mk. 16:1-4; Lk. 24:1-3, 10; Mt. 28:1; Jn. 20:1). *Jerusalem to the Garden Tomb; dawn, Sunday, Apr. 9, 30 A.D.*

394. The women were met by an angel who told them, "He is not here: for he is risen, as he said. Come, see the place where the Lord lay" **(Mt. 28:5-6).** *Near the Garden Tomb; dawn, Sunday, Apr. 9, 30 A.D.*

395. The women found the tomb empty and two angels inside who asked, "Why seek ye the living among the dead?" "He is risen." "Go . . . tell his disciples and Peter that he goeth before you into Galilee" **(Lk. 24:4-8; Mk. 16:5-7; Mt. 28:7; Jn. 20:11-13).** *The Garden Tomb; dawn, Sunday, Apr. 9, 30 A.D.*

396. The women left the tomb and sought the apostles. Mary Magdalene told Peter and John the tomb was empty. They ran to see, believed in the resurrection, and returned to their home (Jn. 20:2-10; Lk. 24:10-12). *Garden Tomb to Jerusalem back to the tomb; dawn, Sunday, Apr. 9, 30 A.D.*

397. Jesus appeared to Mary Magdalene at the tomb. He told her, "Touch me not; for I am not yet ascended to my Father: but go to my brethren, and say unto them, I ascend unto my Father" **(Jn. 20:14-17; Mk. 16:9).** *Outside the Garden Tomb; after dawn, Sunday, Apr. 9, 30 A.D.*

398. Mary Magdalene told the disciples she had seen Jesus (Mk. 16:10-11). *Garden Tomb to Jerusalem; early morning, Sunday, Apr. 9, 30 A.D.*

399. Jesus appeared to the women: "All hail. . . . Go tell my brethren that they go into Galilee, and there shall they see me" **(Mt. 28:9-10).** *Outside Jerusalem; early morning, Sunday, Apr. 9, 30 A.D.*

400. The chief priests were told all that had happened by the guards. They bribed the guards to say that Jesus' disciples came by night and stole the body (Mt. 28:11-15). *Jerusalem; morning, Sunday, Apr. 9, 30 A.D.*

401. Jesus appeared to two disciples on the road to Emmaus. They walked and talked together. When they arrived, they ate together, and then Jesus vanished out of their sight (Lk. 24:13-31; Mk. 16:12). *On the road to Emmaus (60 furlongs = 2½ miles); afternoon and evening of the same day, Sunday, Apr. 9, 30 A.D.*

402. The two disciples returned to Jerusalem, found the eleven apostles and others gathered together, and reported their experience (Lk. 24:33-35; Mk. 16:13). *Emmaus to Jerusalem; evening of the same day, Sunday, Apr. 9, 30 A.D.*

403. The two disciples were told the Lord had appeared to Peter (Lk. 24:34). [Compare 1 Cor. 15:5] *Jerusalem; evening of the same day, Sunday, Apr. 9, 30 A.D.*

404. Jesus appeared to the apostles and other disciples. He ate with them, gave them the Holy Ghost, and taught them: "Behold my hands and my feet, that it is I myself: handle me, and see; for a spirit hath not flesh and bones, as ye see me have" **(Lk. 24:36-48; Jn. 20:19-23; Mk. 16:14).** *Jerusalem; night of the same day, Sunday, Apr. 9, 30 A.D.* ★

405. Thomas was not present when Jesus appeared. The other disciples told him of Jesus' appearance, but he doubted (Jn. 20:24-25). *Jerusalem; during the following week, Apr. 10-16, 30 A.D.*

406. Jesus appeared eight days later to the apostles. Thomas felt Jesus' wounds and believed in the resurrection. Jesus did other signs in the presence of his disciples (Jn. 20:26-31). *Jerusalem; a week after Jesus' appearance to the assembled disciples, Sunday, Apr. 16, 30 A.D.*

407. Jesus appeared to the disciples at the sea of Tiberias. Jesus told Peter to cast his net on the other side of the boat. He did so and it was filled. Jesus cooked fish for the disciples, then told Peter, "Feed my sheep" **(Jn. 21:1-19).** *The Sea of Galilee; Apr. - May, 30 A.D.*

408. Jesus answered Peter's question about John: "If I will that he tarry till I come, what is that to thee? follow thou me" **(Jn. 21:20-25).** *The Sea of Galilee; the same day, Apr. - May, 30 A.D.* ★

409. Jesus appeared to more than 500 brethren at once (1 Cor. 15:6). *Unknown location; Apr. - May, 30 A.D.*

410. Jesus appeared to the apostle James (1 Cor. 15:7). *Location unknown; Apr. - May, 30 A.D.*

411. Jesus called the eleven to a mountain in Galilee, and instructed them to preach the gospel: "Go ye therefore, and teach all nations, baptizing them in the name of the Father, and of the Son, and of the Holy Ghost" **(Mt. 28:16-20; Mk. 16:15-18).** *Unidentified mountain in Galilee; Apr. - May, 30 A.D.* ★

412. Jesus led the disciples out to Bethany, blessed them, and then ascended to heaven before their eyes. Two angels appeared and said, "This same Jesus, which is taken up from you into heaven, shall so come in like manner as ye have seen him go into heaven" **(Lk. 24:50-51; Acts 1:1-11; Mk. 16:19).** *Jerusalem to Bethany; after 40 days, Thursday, May 18, 30 A.D.* ★

413. The disciples returned to Jerusalem, and were constantly in the temple (Lk. 24:52-53; Acts 1:12). *Bethany to Jerusalem; the same day, Thursday, May 18, 30 A.D.*

414. The apostles went forth, and preached everywhere, confirming the word with signs following (Mk. 16:20).

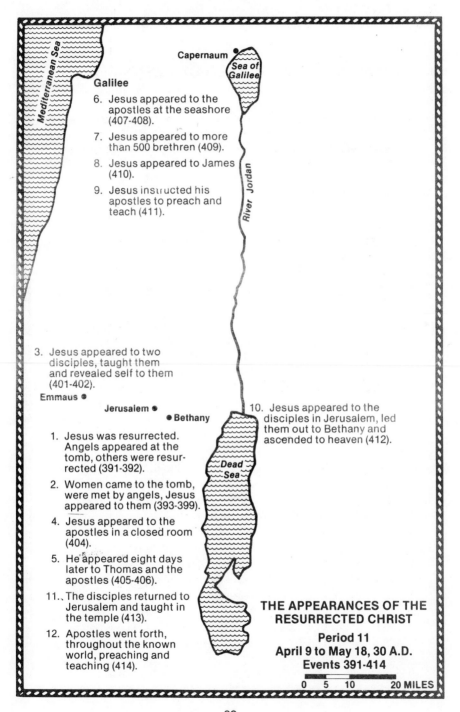

Capernaum

Sea of Galilee

Mediterranean Sea

Galilee

6. Jesus appeared to the apostles at the seashore (407-408).

7. Jesus appeared to more than 500 brethren (409).

8. Jesus appeared to James (410).

9. Jesus instructed his apostles to preach and teach (411).

River Jordan

3. Jesus appeared to two disciples, taught them and revealed self to them (401-402).

Emmaus ●

Jerusalem ●

● Bethany

10. Jesus appeared to the disciples in Jerusalem, led them out to Bethany and ascended to heaven (412).

1. Jesus was resurrected. Angels appeared at the tomb, others were resurrected (391-392).

2. Women came to the tomb, were met by angels, Jesus appeared to them (393-399).

4. Jesus appeared to the apostles in a closed room (404).

5. He appeared eight days later to Thomas and the apostles (405-406).

Dead Sea

11. The disciples returned to Jerusalem and taught in the temple (413).

12. Apostles went forth, throughout the known world, preaching and teaching (414).

THE APPEARANCES OF THE RESURRECTED CHRIST

**Period 11
April 9 to May 18, 30 A.D.
Events 391-414**

0   5   10   20 MILES

THE MAJOR DISCOURSES OF JESUS CHRIST

Listed below are the twenty-four major discourses of Jesus recorded in the four gospels. Many of them actually were answers to questions posed either by his disciples or his antagonists, and treat a variety of unrelated subjects. Embodied in these references, however, are the majority of the Lord's doctrinal teachings.

No.	Event & Period		Reference	Place and Audience
1	54	3	Jn. 3:1-21	Jerusalem, to Nicodemus
2	61	3	Jn. 4:5-27	Jacob's Well, to a Samaritan woman
3	69	4	Lk. 4:16-28	Nazareth, in the synagogue
4	82	4	Mt. 5:1-7:29	Galilee mountain, to his disciples
5	99	4	Lk. 6:17-49	Galilee plain, to his disciples
6	105	4	Jn. 5:17-47	Jerusalem temple, to the Pharisees
7	113	5	Mt. 11:7-30	Galilee, to a multitude
8	124	5	Mt. 12:25-45	Galilee synagogue, to the Pharisees
9	129	5	Mt. 13:3-52	Sea of Galilee, to a multitude
10	170	5	Jn. 6:25-59	Capernaum synagogue, to a multitude
11	202	6	Mt. 18:1-35	Capernaum, to his disciples
12	210	7	Jn. 7:16-39	Jerusalem, to a multitude
13	218	7	Jn. 8:12-59	Jerusalem temple, to the Pharisees
14	225	7	Jn. 10:1-18	Jerusalem, to the Pharisees
15	234	7	Lk. 11:17-52	Judea, to a multitude
16	240	7	Lk. 12:1-59	Judea, to a multitude
17	251	8	Lk. 14:3-24	Peraea, to Pharisees at a feast
18	252	8	Lk. 14:25-17:10	Peraea, to a multitude
19	261	8	Lk. 17:20-18:30	Galilee, to the Pharisees
20	294	9	Mt. 21:23-23:39	Jerusalem temple, to the Pharisees
21	307	9	Jn. 12:20-36	Jerusalem temple, to the Greeks
22	312	9	Mt. 24:3-25:46	Mt. of Olives, to his disciples
23	332	9	Jn. 14:1-16:33	Jerusalem room, to his disciples
24	333	9	Jn. 17:1-26	Jerusalem room, prayer to the Father

A HARMONY OF THE FOUR GOSPELS

The following harmony correlates all events in the life of Jesus Christ as they are listed in this book. The most-detailed account of each event is shown in **bold** type, the others in the standard type face.

Event No.	Event	Yr. & Mo.	Matthew	Mark	Luke	John
Period 1—Christ's Nativity and Preparation (7 B.C. to 26 A.D.)						
1	The preface of St. John					**1:1-14**
2	The preface of St. Luke				**1:1-4**	
3	The genealogies of Christ's mortal parents		**1:1-17**		3:23-38	
4	Birth of John the Baptist foretold to Zacharias Jerusalem	B.C. 7 Oct			**1:5-25**	
5	Zacharias departed to his own house Jerusalem	7 Nov			**1:23**	
6	Elizabeth conceived; months passed Hebron(?)	7 Fall			**1:24-25**	
7	Gabriel foretold the birth of Jesus to Mary Nazareth	6 Jul			**1:26-38**	
8	Mary visited Elizabeth about three months Hebron(?)	6 Smr			1:39-56	
9	Mary returned to Nazareth Nazareth	6 Sep			**1:56**	
10	Birth, circumcision, & naming of John the Baptist Hebron(?)	6 Sep			**1:57-66**	
11	The prophecy of Zacharias Hebron(?)	6 Sep			**1:67-79**	
12	Birth and mission of Jesus foretold to Joseph Nazareth	6 Sep	**1:18-23**			
13	Marriage and relationship of Joseph and Mary		**1:24-25**			
14	The tax decree of Caesar Augustus Rome	6 Fall			**2:1-2**	
15	Joseph and Mary journeyed to Bethlehem Bethlehem	5 Mar			**2:3-5**	
16	The birth of Jesus the Christ Bethlehem	5 Apr	1:25		**2:6-7**	1:14
17	Angels appeared to Bethlehem shepherds near Bethlehem	5 Apr			**2:8-15**	
18	The shepherds visited the baby Jesus Bethlehem	5 Apr			**2:15-20**	
19	The circumcision of Jesus Bethlehem	5 Apr			**2:21**	
20	Jesus was presented in the Jerusalem temple Jerusalem	5 May			**2:22-24**	
21	Simeon came to see Jesus in the temple Jerusalem	5 May			**2:25-35**	
22	The witness of Anna the prophetess Jerusalem	5 May			**2:36-38**	
23	Wise men inquired of King Herod Jerusalem	4	**2:1-8**			
24	Wise men led by a star to Jesus' house Bethlehem(?)	4	**2:9-12**			
25	An angel warned Joseph to flee to Egypt Bethlehem(?)	4	**2:13**			
26	Joseph, Jesus and Mary fled to Egypt Egypt	4 Mar	**2:14-15**			
27	Slaughter of the children of Bethlehem Bethlehem	4	**2:16-18**			
28	Death of Herod the Great Jerusalem	4 Mar	**2:15, 19**			
29	Herod's kingdom divided between his three sons Jerusalem	4				

ATLAS AND OUTLINE OF THE LIFE OF CHRIST

Event No.	Event	Yr. & Mo.	Matthew	Mark	Luke	John
30	Angel instructed Joseph to return to Israel Egypt	4	2:19-20			
31	Joseph, Mary and Jesus journeyed to Nazareth Nazareth	4	2:21-23		2:39	
32	Jesus grew in spirit, wisdom and grace Nazareth	4			2:40	
33	Joseph and Mary attended Passover each year Jerusalem	A.D. Spr			2:41	
34	Jesus' visit to the temple in Jerusalem at twelve Jerusalem	8 Apr			2:42-49	
35	Jesus returned to Nazareth—subject to parents Nazareth	8			2:51	
36	Jesus increased in wisdom, stature and favor Nazareth	8			2:52	

Period 2—Christ's Preliminary Ministry (Summer, 26 A.D. to March-April, 27 A.D.)

Event No.	Event	Yr. & Mo.	Matthew	Mark	Luke	John
37	Political world at time of Jesus' ministry				3:1-2	
38	John preached and baptized near Jordan River Judea	26 Sum	3:1-6	1:1-6	3:3-6	1:15-18(?)
39	John's confrontation with Sadducees, Pharisees Judea	26 Fall	3:7-12	1:7-8	3:7-18	
40	Jesus came from Nazareth to the Jordan River Jordan River	26 Fall	3:13	1:9		
41	Jesus was baptized by John Jordan River	26 Fall	3:14-17	1:9-11	3:21-22	
42	Jesus became 30 years old				3:23	
43	The temptations of Jesus Wilderness	26 Fall	4:1-11	1:12-13	4:1-13	
44	John answered the priests from Jerusalem Bethabara	26 Fall				1:19-28
45	John testified to his followers of Christ Bethabara	26 Fall				1:29-34
46	Jesus met John, Andrew and Simon Peter Sea of Galilee	26 Fall				1:35-42
47	Jesus met Philip and Nathanael Galilee	26 Fall				1:43-51
48	Jesus turned water into wine at marriage Cana	26 Fall				2:1-11
49	Jesus stayed in Capernaum with family Capernaum	27 Mar				2:12

Period 3—Christ's Early Judean Ministry (April, 27 A.D. to December, 27 A.D.)

Event No.	Event	Yr. & Mo.	Matthew	Mark	Luke	John
50	Jesus went to Jerusalem for first Passover Jerusalem	27 Apr				2:13
51	Jesus drove merchants and animals from temple Jerusalem	27 Apr				2:14-17
52	Jesus answered the Jews who asked for a sign Jerusalem	27 Apr				2:18-22
53	Jesus did many miracles during Passover Jerusalem	27 Apr				2:23-25
54	Jesus taught Nicodemus Jerusalem	27 Apr				3:1-21
55	Jesus tarried and baptized in Judea Judea	27 Sum				3:22
56	John the Baptist also baptized farther north Aenon	27 Sum				3:23-24
57	John testified to his disciples about Christ Aenon	27 Sum				3:25-36
58	Herod imprisoned John the Baptist Machaerus	27 Sum	14:3-5	6:17-20	3:19-20	
59	Jesus baptized more disciples than John Judea	27 Fall				4:1-2
60	Jesus left Judea for Galilee through Samaria	27 Dec	4:12	1:14		4:3
61	Jesus taught Samaritan woman at Jacob's well Samaria	27 Dec				4:5-27

92

Event No.	Event	Yr. & Mo.	Matthew	Mark	Luke	John
62	Samaritan woman brought others to meet Jesus Sychar	27 Dec				4:28-30
63	Jesus taught his disciples at Jacob's well Sychar	27 Dec				4:31-38
64	Jesus stayed two days with Samaritans at Sychar Sychar	27 Dec				4:39-42
65	Jesus and his disciples went to Galilee Galilee	27 Dec				4:43-45

Period 4—Christ's Early Galilean Ministry (December, 27 A.D. to April, 28 A.D.)

Event No.	Event	Yr. & Mo.	Matthew	Mark	Luke	John
66	Jesus went again to Cana Cana	28 Wtr				4:46
67	Jesus healed the nobleman's son Cana	28 Wtr				4:46-54
68	Jesus taught in the synagogues of Galilee Galilee	27 Wtr			4:14-15	
69	Jesus preached in the synagogue at Nazareth Nazareth	28 Wtr			4:16-28	
70	Nazareth rejected Jesus and tried to kill him Nazareth	28 Wtr			4:29-30	
71	Jesus left Nazareth and dwelt in Capernaum Capernaum	28 Wtr	4:13-16			
72	Jesus began to preach Capernaum	28 Wtr	4:17	1:15		
73	Jesus called Peter and Andrew back to work Sea of Galilee	28 Wtr	4:18-20	1:16-18		
74	Jesus called James and John to leave ships Capernaum	28 Wtr	4:21-22	1:19-20		
75	Jesus went to Capernaum and taught there Capernaum	28 Wtr		1:21-22	4:31-32	
76	Jesus healed a Demoniac in the synagogue Capernaum	28 Wtr		1:23-28	4:33-37	
77	Jesus healed Simon Peter's mother-in-law Capernaum	28 Wtr	8:14-15	1:29-31	4:38-39	
78	Jesus healed many and cast out many devils Capernaum	28 Wtr	8:16-17	1:32-34	4:40-41	
79	Jesus prayed in the desert before sunrise Capernaum	28 Wtr		1:35-38	4:42-43	
80	Jesus preached throughout Galilee Galilee	28 Spr	4:23	1:39	4:44	
81	Jesus' fame spread throughout Syria Galilee	28 Spr	4:24-25			
82	Jesus gave his Sermon on the Mount Galilee area	28 Spr	5:1-7:29			
83	Jesus healed a leper Galilee	28 Spr	8:1-4	1:40-45	5:12-15	
84	Jesus taught a crowd from Simon's boat Sea of Galilee	28 Spr			5:1-3	
85	Jesus helped disciples catch draught of fishes Sea of Galilee	28 Spr			5:4-11	
86	Jesus withdrew into the wilderness to pray Galilee	28 Spr			5:16	
87	Jesus healed a palsied man lowered through roof Capernaum	28 Spr	9:2-8	2:1-12	5:17-26	
88	Jesus taught the multitudes by the seaside Sea of Galilee	28 Spr		2:13		
89	Jesus called Levi (Matthew), the tax collector Capernaum	28 Spr	9:9	2:14	5:27-28	
90	Jesus answered scribes at Levi's feast Capernaum	28 Spr	9:10-13	2:15-17	5:29-32	
91	Jesus answered John's disciples about fasting Capernaum	28 Spr	9:14-17	2:18-22	5:33-39	
92	Disciples plucked corn on the Sabbath day Galilee	28 Spr	12:1-8	2:23-28	6:1-5	
93	Jesus healed man's withered hand in synagogue Galilee	28 Spr	12:9-13	3:1-5	6:6-10	
94	Pharisees and Herodians plotted Jesus' death ------	28 Spr	12:14	3:6	6:11	
95	Jesus and his disciples withdrew to the sea Sea of Galilee	28 Spr	12:15-21	3:7-8		

Event No.	Event	Yr. & Mo.	Matthew	Mark	Luke	John
96	Jesus spoke from a boat Sea of Galilee	28 Spr		3:9-12		
97	Jesus prayed all night on the mountain Galilee	28 Spr			6:12	
98	Jesus ordained his twelve apostles Galilee	28 Spr		3:13-19	6:13-16	
99	Jesus delivered his Sermon on the Plain Capernaum	28 Spr			6:17-49	
100	Jesus attended a Jerusalem feast (Passover?) Jerusalem	28 Apr				5:1
101	Jesus healed impotent man by pool of Bethesda Jerusalem	28 Apr				5:2-9
102	The Jews rebuked the man Jesus healed Jerusalem	28 Apr				5:10-13
103	Jesus talked to the man he healed in the temple Jerusalem	28 Apr				5:14
104	Man Jesus healed testified of Jesus to Jews Jerusalem	28 Apr				5:15-16
105	Jesus testified of his divine Sonship to Jews Jerusalem	28 Apr				5:17-47
106	Jesus returned to Galilee Galilee	28 Apr				

Period 5—Christ's Great Galilean Ministry (April, 28 A.D. to April, 29 A.D.)

Event No.	Event	Yr. & Mo.	Matthew	Mark	Luke	John
107	Jesus went to Capernaum Capernaum	28 Spr	8:5		7:1	
108	Jesus healed a Roman centurion's servant Capernaum	28 Spr	8:5-13		7:2-10	
109	Jesus went to Nain with his disciples Nain	28 Spr			7:11	
110	Jesus raised a widow's son from the dead Nain	28 Spr			7:12-17	
111	John the Baptist told of Christ's deeds Machaerus	28 Sum			7:18	
112	Messengers from John the Baptist met Jesus Galilee	28 Sum	11:2-6		7:19-23	
113	A discourse about John the Baptist Galilee	28 Sum	11:7-15		7:24-28	
114	Disciples of John the Baptist accepted Jesus Galilee	28 Sum			7:29-30	
115	Jesus replied to Pharisees' criticism Galilee	28 Sum	11:16-19		7:31-35	
116	Jesus upbraided the cities of Galilee Galilee	28 Sum	11:20-24			
117	Jesus prayed to his Father Galilee	28 Sum	11:25-27			
118	Jesus invited mankind to take his yoke Galilee	28 Sum	11:28-30			
119	Jesus ate at the home of Simon the Pharisee Galilee	28 Fall			7:36	
120	A woman anointed Jesus' feet with oil Galilee	28 Fall			7:37-39	
121	Jesus commended the woman who anointed him Galilee	28 Fall			7:40-50	
122	The mission through Galilee with the Twelve Galilee	28 Fall			8:1-3	
123	Jesus healed a blind and dumb Demonic man Capernaum(?)	28 Fall	12:22-23			
124	Jesus charged with working with the Devil Capernaum(?)	28 Fall	12:24-37	3:22-30		
125	Jesus' discourse on signs Capernaum(?)	28 Fall	12:38-45			
126	Jesus' mother and brothers came to seek him Capernaum(?)	28 Fall	12:46-50	3:31-35	8:19-21	
127	Jesus taught again from a boat Sea of Galilee	28 Fall	13:1-3	4:1-2	8:4	
128	Parable of the sower Sea of Galilee	28 Fall	13:3-9	4:3-9	8:5-8	
129	Jesus explained why he taught in parables Sea of Galilee	28 Fall	13:10-17	4:10-12	8:9-10	

A HARMONY OF THE FOUR GOSPELS

Event No.	Event	Yr. & Mo.	Matthew	Mark	Luke	John
130	Jesus interpreted the parable of the sower Sea of Galilee	28 Fall	13:18-23	4:13-20	8:11-15	
131	Parable of the candle under a bushel Sea of Galilee	28 Fall		4:21-25	8:16-18	
132	Parable of the seed growing secretly Sea of Galilee	28 Fall		4:26-29		
133	Parable of the tares of the field Sea of Galilee	28 Fall	13:24-30			
134	Parable of the mustard seed Sea of Galilee	28 Fall	13:31-32	4:30-32		
135	Parable of the hidden leaven Sea of Galilee	28 Fall	13:33			
136	Jesus spoke only in parables to the multitudes Sea of Galilee	28 Fall	13:34-35	4:33-34		
137	Parable of the tares explained Capernaum(?)	28 Fall	13:36-43			
138	Parable of the treasure hidden in the field Capernaum(?)	28 Fall	13:44			
139	Parable of the pearl of great price Capernaum(?)	28 Fall	13:45-46			
140	Parable of the net that gathered every kind Capernaum(?)	28 Fall	13:47-50			
141	Parable of the scribe in the kingdom Capernaum(?)	28 Fall	13:51-52			
142	Jesus discussed discipleship with a scribe Capernaum(?)	28 Fall	8:18-20			
143	Jesus told a disciple to "let the dead bury ..." Capernaum(?)	28 Fall	8:21-22			
144	Jesus calmed a storm on the sea Sea of Galilee	28 Fall	8:23-27	4:35-41	8:22-25	
145	Jesus cast demons out of men into swine Gergesa	28 Fall	8:28-34	5:1-13	8:26-33	
146	The people of Gergesa asked Jesus to depart Gergesa	28 Fall	8:33-34	5:16-17	8:34-37	
147	Jesus sent a healed man back to Gergesa Gergesa	28 Fall		5:18-20	8:38-39	
148	Jesus and his disciples returned to Capernaum to Capernaum	28 Fall	9:1	5:21	8:40	
149	Jairus asked Jesus to heal his daughter Capernaum	28 Fall	9:18-19	5:22-24	8:41-42	
150	The woman with the issue of blood healed Capernaum	28 Fall	9:20-22	5:25-34	8:43-48	
151	Jesus raised the daughter of Jairus Capernaum	28 Fall	9:23-26	5:35-43	8:49-56	
152	Jesus healed two blind men Capernaum	28 Fall	9:27-31			
153	Jesus healed dumb man possessed with a devil Capernaum	28 Fall	9:32-33			
154	The second rejection at Nazareth Nazareth	28 Wtr	13:54-58	6:1-6		
155	Jesus again traveled through Galilee Galilee	29 Wtr	9:35-38			
156	Jesus sent out 12 apostles two-by-two to preach Galilee	28 Wtr		6:7-13	9:1-6	
157	Jesus continued to teach throughout Galilee Galilee	29 Wtr	11:1			
158	Herod had John beheaded Machaerus	29 Wtr	14:3-12	6:17-29		
159	Herod thought Jesus was John Tiberias	29 Wtr	14:1-2	6:14-16	9:7-9	
160	The Twelve returned & reported on their missions Galilee	29 Wtr		6:30	9:10	
161	John the Baptist's death reported to Jesus Galilee	29 Apr	14:12			
162	Jesus and disciples went by ship to Bethsaida to Bethsaida	29 Apr	14:13	6:31-32	9:10	
163	People ran and met Jesus on the other side Bethsaida	29 Apr	14:14	6:33-34	9:11	
164	Jesus multiplied bread and fishes to feed 5,000 Bethsaida	29 Apr	14:14-21	6:35-44	9:11-17	6:1-14

Event No.	Event	Yr. & Mo.	Matthew	Mark	Luke	John
165	Jesus prevented their making him king Galilee	29 Apr	14:22-23	6:45-46		6:15
166	Jesus went alone to a mountain to pray Bethsaida	29 Apr	14:23	6:46		6:15
167	Jesus walked on the water to disciples' ship Sea of Galilee	29 Apr	14:24-33	6:47-52		6:16-21
168	The multitudes found Jesus in Gennesaret Gennesaret	29 Apr	14:34	6:53		6:22-25
169	People in the land of Gennesaret healed Gennesaret	28 Apr	14:35-36	6:54-56		
170	Jesus called himself "the bread of life" Capernaum	29 Apr				6:25-59
171	Many disciples being offended, left him Capernaum	29 Apr				6:60-66
172	Jesus gave the Twelve the chance to leave also Capernaum	29 Apr				6:67-71
173	Jesus rebuked a group of scribes and Pharisees Capernaum(?)	29 Apr	15:1-9	7:1-13		
174	Jesus explained the principle of cleanliness Capernaum(?)	29 Apr	15:10-11	7:14-16		
175	Pharisees called "blind leading the blind" Capernaum(?)	29 Apr	15:12-14			
176	Jesus further explained cleanliness Capernaum	29 Apr	15:15-20	7:17-23		
177	Jesus did not attend Passover in Jerusalem Jerusalem	29 Apr				

Period 6—Christ's Late Galilean Ministry (April, 29 A.D. to October, 29 A.D.)

Event No.	Event	Yr. & Mo.	Matthew	Mark	Luke	John
178	Jesus and his disciples went to Tyre and Sidon to Tyre, Sidon	29 Spr	15:21	7:24		7:1
179	Jesus cast devil out of a Syrophoenician girl Sidon(?)	29 Sum	25:22-28	7:24-30		
180	Jesus left Phoenicia for Galilee to Galilee	29 Sum	15:29	7:31		
181	A multitude met Jesus on a mountain Galilee	29 Sum	15:30-32			
182	Jesus healed deaf man with speech impediment Galilee	29 Sum		7:32-37		
183	Jesus fed 4,000 plus with loaves and fishes Galilee	29 Sum	15:32-38	8:1-9		
184	Jesus left the multitude and sailed to Magdala to Magdala	29 Sum	15:39	8:10		
185	Pharisees and Sadducees asked for a sign Magdala	29 Sum	16:1-4	8:11-13		
186	Jesus and his disciples sailed to Bethsaida	29	16:5	8:13		
187	Disciples warned about Pharisees and Sadducees Sea of Galilee	29 Sum	16:5-12	8:14-21		
188	Jesus healed a blind man in Bethsaida Bethsaida	29 Sum		8:22-26		
189	Jesus and his disciples visited Caesarea Philippi to Caesarea Philippi	29 Fall	16:13	8:27		
190	Jesus gave Peter the keys of the kingdom Caesarea Philippi	29 Fall	16:13-20	8:27-30	9:18-21	
191	Jesus prophesied of his death in Jerusalem Caesarea Philippi	29 Fall	16:21-22	8:31	9:22	
192	Jesus rebuked Peter Caesarea Philippi	29 Fall	16:22-23	8:32-33		
193	Jesus taught disciples to deny themselves Caesarea Philippi	29 Fall	16:24-27	8:34-38	9:23-26	
194	Jesus prophesied that some would not die Caesarea Philippi	29 Fall	16:28	9:1	9:27	
195	The transfiguration of Christ, Moses Elias Mt. Hermon	29 Fall	17:1-9	9:2-10	9:28-36	
196	Jesus explained the role of John the Baptist Mt. Hermon(?)	29 Fall	17:10-13	9:11-13		
197	Jesus healed lunatic boy, disciples couldn't Caesarea Philippi	29 Fall	17:14-18	9 ;14-27	9:37-42	
198	Jesus explained about casting out devils Caesarea Philippi	29 Fall	17:19-21	9:28-29		

96

Event No.	Event	Yr. & Mo.	Matthew	Mark	Luke	John
199	Jesus traveled to Capernaum to Capernaum	29 Fall		**9:30**		
200	Jesus taught of his death and resurrection to Capernaum	29 Fall	17:22-23	**9:31-32**	9:43-45	
201	Peter paid tax with money from fish's mouth Capernaum	29 Fall	**17:24-27**			
202	Jesus taught to become as a little child Capernaum	29 Fall	**18:1-20**	9:33-37	9:46-48	
203	Jesus taught "He that is not against us . . ." Capernaum	29 Fall		**9:38-41**	9:49-50	
204	Jesus taught to forgive seventy times seven Capernaum	29 Fall	**18:21-35**			
205	Jesus refused to call down fire on Samaritans Capernaum	29 Fall			9:51-56	
206	Jesus taught importance of not looking back Capernaum	29 Fall			9:57-62	
207	Jesus refused to go to feast of tabernacles Galilee	29 Fall				7:2-9
208	Jesus went in secret to the feast of tabernacles to Jerusalem	29 Oct				7:10

Period 7—Christ's Late Judean Ministry (October, 29 A.D. to December, 29 A.D.)

Event No.	Event	Yr. & Mo.	Matthew	Mark	Luke	John
209	The Jews sought Jesus at the feast of tabernacles Jerusalem	29 Oct				7:11-13
210	Jesus taught in the temple Jerusalem	29 Oct				7:14-31
211	Officers went to the temple to arrest Jesus Jerusalem	29 Oct				7:32
212	Jesus preached on the last day of the feast Jerusalem	29 Oct				7:37-39
213	People debated whether Jesus was the Christ Jerusalem	29 Oct				7:40-44
214	Officers were rebuked for not arresting Jesus Jerusalem	29 Oct				7:45-49
215	Nicodemus spoke to priest in defense of Jesus Jerusalem	29 Oct				7:50-53
216	Jesus went to the Mount of Olives Jerusalem	29 Oct				8:1
217	Jesus judged a woman caught in adultery Jerusalem	29 Oct				8:2-11
218	Jesus taught "I am the light of the world" Jerusalem	29 Oct				8:12-59
219	Jesus healed a man born blind Jerusalem	29 Oct				9:1-12
220	Pharisees questioned the healed blind man Jerusalem	29 Oct				9:18-23
221	Pharisees interviewed parents of healed man Jerusalem	29 Oct				9:18-23
222	Blind man again interviewed, then cast out Jerusalem	29 Oct				9:24-34
223	Jesus spoke to him, said he is the Son of God Jerusalem	29 Oct				9:35-38
224	Jesus told Pharisees he was to judge Jerusalem	29 Oct				9:39-41
225	Jesus said "I am the good shepherd" Jerusalem	29 Oct				10:18
226	Pharisees thought Jesus mad or possessed Jerusalem	29 Oct				10:19-21
227	Jesus appointed the seventy to preach Jerusalem(?)	29 Oct			10:1-16	
228	The seventy returned from preaching Jerusalem(?)	29 Fall			10:17-20	
229	Jesus prayed and gave thanks to his Father Jerusalem(?)	29 Fall			10:21-22	
230	Jesus told disciples they were blessed to see Jerusalem(?)	29 Fall			10:23-24	
231	Jesus taught "Love the Lord thy God . . ." Jerusalem(?)	29 Fall			10:25-37	
232	Jesus visited Mary and Martha in Bethany Bethany	29 Fall			10:38-42	

Event No.	Event	Yr. & Mo.	Matthew	Mark	Luke	John
233	Jesus gave his disciples the Lord's Prayer Judea	29 Fall			11:1-13	
234	Jesus cast a devil out of a dumb man Judea	29 Fall			11:14-26	
235	Jesus blessed those who keep the word of God Judea	29 Fall			11:27-28	
236	Jesus taught about darkness and light Judea	29 Fall			11:29-36	
237	Jesus reproved the Pharisees for worldliness Judea	29 Fall			11:37-44	
238	Jesus criticized the Lawyers Judea	29 Fall			11:45-52	
239	Many provoked Jesus so they could accuse him Judea	29 Fall			11:53-54	
240	Jesus said "Seek ye first the kingdom of God" Judea	29 Fall			12:1-59	
241	Jesus explained that death is not a sign of sin Judea	29 Fall			13:1-10	
242	Jesus healed a woman bowed over for 18 years Judea	29 Fall			13:11-13	
243	Jesus defended his healing on the Sabbath day Judea	29 Fall			13:14-17	
244	Jesus made comparisons to the kingdom of God Judea	29 Fall			13:18-21	
245	Jesus taught as he journeyed to Jerusalem to Jerusalem	29 Dec			13:22	
246	Jesus attended the feast of dedication Jerusalem	29 Dec			10:22	
247	Jews attempted to stone Jesus Jerusalem	29 Dec				10:23-29

Period 8—Christ's Perean Ministry (January 30 A.D. to April, 30 A.D.)

Event No.	Event	Yr. & Mo.	Matthew	Mark	Luke	John
248	Jesus went beyond Jordan—many followed to Peraea	30 Jan				10:30-42
249	Jesus taught "Enter in at the strait gate ..." Peraea	30 Wtr			13:23-30	
250	Jesus warned to leave or Herod would kill him Peraea	30 Wtr			13:31-35	
251	Parable of the marriage supper Peraea	30 Wtr			14:1-24	
252	Jesus taught another great day of parables Peraea	30 Wtr			14:25-17:10	
253	Jesus received word that Lazarus was sick Peraea	30 Wtr				11:1-5
254	Jesus waited two days, then went to Bethany to Bethany	30 Wtr				11:6-17
255	Jesus comforted Mary and Martha outside of town Bethany	30 Wtr				11:18-37
256	Jesus brought Lazarus back from the dead Bethany	30 Wtr				11:38-45
257	Council of the Pharisees and chief priests Jerusalem	30 Wtr				11:46-53
258	Jesus went into hiding in Ephriam to Ephriam	30 Feb				11:54
259	Jesus began his final journey to Jerusalem to Jerusalem	30 Feb			17:11	
260	Jesus healed ten lepers, only one thanked him Galilee	30 Feb			17:12-19	
261	Jesus said "The kingdom of God is within you" Galilee	30 Mar			17:20-21	
262	Jesus prophesied of his coming in glory Galilee	30 Mar			17:22-37	
263	Parable of the importunate widow Galilee	30 Mar			18:1-8	
264	Parable of the Pharisee and the Publican Galilee	30 Mar			18:9-14	
265	Jesus taught in Perea Peraea	30 Mar	19:1-2	10:1		
266	Jesus taught about divorce Peraea	30 Mar	19:3-9	10:2-9		

Event No.	Event	Yr. & Mo.	Matthew	Mark	Luke	John
267	Jesus taught more concerning divorce Peraea	30 Mar	**19:10-12**	10:10-12		
268	Jesus said "Suffer the little children . . ." Peraea	30 Mar	19:13-15	**10:13-16**	18:15-17	
269	Jesus advised rich ruler to sell all and follow Peraea	30 Mar	19:16-22	**10:17-22**	18:18-23	
270	Difficulty of Rich entering heaven discussed Peraea	30 Mar	19:23-26	**10:23-27**	18:24-27	
271	Jesus promised the 12 apostles many blessings Peraea	30 Mar	**19:27-30**	10:28-31	18:28-30	
272	Parable of the laborers in the vineyard Peraea	30 Mar	**20:1-16**			
273	Jesus prophesied again of his death & resurrection Peraea	30 Mar	20:17-19	**10:32-34**	18:31-34	
274	James and John asked Jesus for extra glory Jericho(?)	30 Mar	20:20-28	**10:35-45**		
275	Jesus healed blind Bartimaeus Jericho	30 Mar	20:29-34	**10:46-52**	18:35-43	
276	Parable of the ten pounds given to Zacchaeus Jericho	30 Mar			**19:1-7**	
277	Jesus ascended up to Jerusalem to Jerusalem	30 Apr			**19:28**	
278	Jews sought Jesus before Passover Jerusalem	30 Apr				**11:55-56**
279	Chief priests started a search for Jesus Jerusalem	30 Apr				**11:57**
280	Jesus came to Bethany to Bethany	30 Apr				**12:1**

Period 9—Christ's Preparation for His Atoning Sacrifice
(Sunday, April 2, 30 A.D. to Thursday, April 6, 30 A.D.)

Event No.	Event	Yr. & Mo.	Matthew	Mark	Luke	John
281	Jesus sent disciples to bring ass for him Mt. of Olives	30 Apr	21:1-6	**11:1-6**	19:29-34	
282	Jesus' triumphal entry into Jerusalem Jerusalem	30 Apr	21:7-11	11:7-10	19:35-38	**12:12-18**
283	Jesus refused to rebuke disciples' rejoicing Jerusalem	30 Apr			**19:39-40**	12:19
284	Jesus wept for Jerusalem Jerusalem	30 Apr			19:41-44	
285	Jesus healed the sick and taught in the temple Jerusalem	30 Apr	**21:14**		19:47	
286	Pharisees objected to Jesus' miracles Jerusalem	30 Apr	**21:15-16**			
287	Jesus reentered Jerusalem and the temple Jerusalem	30 Apr		**11:11**		
288	Jesus and his disciples went to lodge in Bethany to Bethany	30 Apr	**21:17**	11:11		
289	Jesus and his disciples returned to Jerusalem to Jerusalem	30 Apr	21:18	**11:12**		
290	Jesus cursed a barren fig tree to Jerusalem	30 Apr	21:19	**11:12-14**		
291	Jesus again cast moneychangers out of the temple Jerusalem	30 Apr	21:12-13	**11:15-17**	19:45-46	
292	Jesus returned to Bethany to Bethany	30 Apr		**11:19**		
293	Jesus commented on prayer and forgiveness to Jerusalem	30 Apr	21:20-22	**11:20-26**		
294	Chief priests questioned Jesus' authority Jerusalem	30 Apr	**21:23-27**	11:27-33	20:1-8	
295	Parable of the two sons Jerusalem	30 Apr	**21:28-32**			
296	Parable of the wicked husbandmen Jerusalem	30 Apr	**21:33-41**	12:1-9	20:9-16	
297	Jesus prophesied the captivity of Jerusalem Jerusalem	30 Apr	**21:42-44**	12:10-11	20:17-18	
298	The Pharisees were afraid to arrest Jesus Jerusalem	30 Apr	**21:45-46**	12:12	20:19	
299	Parable of the marriage of the king's son Jerusalem	30 Apr	**22:1-14**			

Event No.	Event	Yr. & Mo.	Matthew	Mark	Luke	John
300	Some attempted to catch Jesus in his words Jerusalem	30 Apr	**22:15-22**	12:13-17	20:20-26	
301	Jesus taught about marriage after death Jerusalem	30 Apr	**22:23-33**	12:18-27	20:27-40	
302	Jesus taught first and second great commandments Jerusalem	30 Apr	22:35-40	**12:28-34**		
303	Christ, the son of David, called Lord Jerusalem	30 Apr	**22:41-46**	12:35-37	20:41-44	
304	Christ denounced scribes as hypocrites Jerusalem	30 Apr	**23:1-26**	12:38-40	20:45-47	
305	Jesus lamented over Jerusalem Jerusalem	30 Apr	**23:37-39**			
306	Jesus praised the widow's contribution Jerusalem	30 Apr		**12:41-44**	21:1-4	
307	A voice from heaven answered Jesus in the temple Jerusalem	30 Apr				**12:20-36**
308	Jesus departed and hid himself Jerusalem	30 Apr				**12:36**
309	Many did not believe Jesus Jerusalem	30 Apr				**12:37-43**
310	Jesus taught his relationship with the Father Jerusalem	30 Apr				**12:44-50**
311	Jesus prophesied destruction of the temple Jerusalem	30 Apr	**24:1-2**	13:1-2	21:5-6	
312	Jesus gave his Olivet discourse Mt. of Olives	30 Apr	**24:3-51**	13:3-37	21:7-36	
313	Parable of the ten virgins Mt. of Olives	30 Apr	**25:1-13**			
314	Parable of the talents Mt. of Olives	30 Apr	**25:14-30**			
315	Jesus prophesied of the final judgment Mt. of Olives	30 Apr	**25:31-33**			
316	Jesus taught about service Mt. of Olives	30 Apr	**25:34-46**			
317	Jesus foretold his death Mt. of Olives	30 Apr	**26:1-2**			
318	Chief priests met to plot Jesus' death Jerusalem	30 Apr	**26:3-5**	14:1-2	22:1-2	
319	Jesus returned to Bethany to Bethany	30 Apr	**26:6**	14:3		
320	Mary anointed Jesus at Simon's supper Bethany	30 Apr	26:6-13	14:3-9		**12:2-9**
321	Christ taught at the temple Jerusalem	30 Apr			21:37-38	
322	Judas Iscariot covenanted to betray Jesus Jerusalem	30 Apr	**26:14-16**	14:10-11	22:3-6	
323	Peter and John were sent to find room for supper Jerusalem	30 Apr	26:17-19	14:12-16	**22:7-13**	
324	Jesus and the Twelve ate meal in the upper room Jerusalem	30 Apr	**26:20**	14:17-18	22:14	
325	Passover meal—The Last Supper Jerusalem	30 Apr			**22:15-18**	
326	Institution of sacrament of the Lord's Supper Jerusalem	30 Apr	**26:26-29**	14:22-25	22:19-20	
327	Jesus washed the feet of his disciples Jerusalem	30 Apr				**13:2-15**
328	Jesus told his disciples to serve each other Jerusalem	30 Apr			22:24-30	13:13-17
329	Jesus indicated Judas would betray him Jerusalem	30 Apr	**26:21-25**	14:18-21	22:21-23	13:18-26
330	Judas left to betray Jesus Jerusalem	30 Apr				**13:27-30**
331	Peter declared his loyalty to Jesus Jerusalem	30 Apr			22:31-34	13:36-38
332	Jesus taught about the Comforter Jerusalem	30 Apr				**14:1-16:33**
333	Jesus prayed for his followers Jerusalem	30 Apr				**17:1-26**
334	They sang a hymn and went to the Mt. of Olives Mt. of Olives	30 Apr	**26:30**	14:26	22:39	

A HARMONY OF THE FOUR GOSPELS

No.	Event	Yr. & Mo.	Matthew	Mark	Luke	John
335	Jesus told disciples they would be offended Mt. of Olives	30 Apr	**26:31-35**	14:27-31		
336	Jesus went to Gethsemane to pray Mt. of Olives	30 Apr	**26:36-37**	14:32-33		18:1
337	The agony in the Garden of Gethsemane Mt. of Olives	30 Apr	26:38-46	14:34-42	**22:40-46**	
338	Judas Iscariot betrayed Jesus with a kiss Mt. of Olives	30 Apr	26:47-50	14:43-46	22:47-48	**18:2-9**
339	Jesus healed a man injured by Peter Mt. of Olives	30 Apr	26:51-54	14:47	22:50-51	**18:10-11**
340	Jesus rebuked his captors Mt. of Olives	30 Apr	**26:55-56**	14:48-49	22:52-54	
341	All of his disciples forsook Jesus and fled Mt. of Olives	30 Apr	26:56	**14:50-52**		
342	Jesus was bound and led away Mt. of Olives	30 Apr				**18:12-13**

Period 10—Christ's Trial, Crucifixion and Burial
(Early Friday Morning, April 17, 30 A.D. to Early Sunday Morning, April 9, 30 A.D.)

No.	Event	Yr. & Mo.	Matthew	Mark	Luke	John
343	Jesus was taken before Annas Jerusalem	30 Apr				**18:13-14**
344	Annas sent Jesus to Caiaphas, the high priest Jerusalem	30 Apr	26:57-58	**14:53-54**	22:54	18:24
345	Caiaphas questioned Jesus about his doctrines Jerusalem	30 Apr				**18:19-23**
346	Jesus was sentenced to death by Jewish court Jerusalem	30 Apr	26:59-66	**14:55-64**		
347	Jewish guards mocked and struck Jesus Jerusalem	30 Apr	26:67-68	14:65	**22:63-64**	
348	Peter three times denied being a disciple Jerusalem	30 Apr	**26:69-75**	14:66-72	22:55-62	18:25-27
349	The Sanhedrin met and upheld their verdict Jerusalem	30 Apr	**27:1**	15:1	22:66-71	
350	The multitude took Jesus to the Hall of Judgment Jerusalem	30 Apr	**27:2**	15:1	23:1	18:28
351	Judas returned the money, then hanged himself Jerusalem	30 Apr	**27:3-10**			
352	Pilate tried Jesus and found no fault in him Jerusalem	30 Apr	27:11-14	15:2-5	23:2-5	**18:28-38**
353	Pilate sent Jesus to Herod, who returned him Jerusalem	30 Apr			**23:7-12**	
354	The Jews would not let Pilate free Jesus Jerusalem	30 Apr	**27:15-23**	15:6-14	23:13-23	18:39-40
355	Pilate's wife sent a message to free Jesus Jerusalem	30 Apr	**27:19**			
356	Pilate symbolicly washed his hands of guilt Jerusalem	30 Apr	**27:24-25**			
357	Pilate sentenced Jesus to death Jerusalem	30 Apr			**23:24**	
358	Pilate returned Barabbas to the multitude Jerusalem	30 Apr	**27:26**	15:15	23:25	
359	Jesus was scourged Jerusalem	30 Apr	**27:26**	15:15		19:1
360	Roman soldiers mocked Jesus in the Praetorium Jerusalem	30 Apr	**27:27-30**	15:16-19		19:2-3
361	Pilate again brought Jesus before the crowd Jerusalem	30 Apr				**19:4-7**
362	Pilate again questioned Jesus Jerusalem	30 Apr				**19:8-12**
363	Pilate said "Behold your king!" Jerusalem	30 Apr				**19:13-16**
364	Jesus was led away to be crucified Jerusalem	30 Apr	**27:31**	15:20		19:16
365	Simon, from Cyrene, forced to carry the cross Jerusalem	30 Apr	27:32	15:21	**23:26**	
366	A great company followed Jesus, mourning Jerusalem	30 Apr			**23:27-31**	
367	They came to Calvary (Golgotha) to Golgotha	20 Apr	27:33	15:22	**23:33**	19:17

Event No.	Event	Yr. & Mo.	Matthew	Mark	Luke	John
368	Jesus refused vinegar and gall to drink Golgotha	30 Apr	**27:34**	15:23		
369	Jesus was crucified between two thieves Golgotha	30 Apr	27:35, 38	15:24-28	**23:32-33**	19:18
370	A title was placed above Jesus on the cross Golgotha	30 Apr	27:37	15:26	23:37-38	**19:19-22**
371	The soldiers divided his garments among them Golgotha	30 Apr	27:35-36	15:24	23:34	**19:23-24**
372	Jesus said "Father, forgive them . . ." Golgotha	30 Apr			**23:34**	
373	The multitude and thieves mocked Jesus Golgotha	30 Apr	**27:39-44**	15:29-32	23:35-37	
374	Jesus gave a promise to the thief beside him Golgotha	30 Apr			**23:39-43**	
375	Jesus instructed John to care for his mother Golgotha	30 Apr				**19:25-27**
376	Darkness covered the earth for three hours Golgotha	30 Apr	27:45	15:33	**23:44-45**	
377	Jesus said "My God, why has thou forsaken me?" Golgotha	30 Apr	**27:46-47**	15:34-35		
378	Jesus stated "I thirst." Golgotha	30 Apr	27:48-49	15:36		**19:28-29**
379	Jesus said "It is finished." Golgotha	30 Apr				**19:30**
380	Jesus said "Father, into thy hands . . ." Golgotha	30 Apr			**23:46**	
381	Jesus bowed his head and gave up the ghost Golgotha	30 Apr	27:50	15:37	23:46	**19:30**
382	The veil in the temple was rent Jerusalem	30 Apr	**27:51**	15:38	23:45	
383	The watching soldiers were frightened Golgotha	30 Apr	**27:54**	15:39	23:47	
384	Many women followers of Christ were watching Golgotha	30 Apr	**27:55-56**	15:40-41	23:49	
385	The soldiers pierced Jesus' side Golgotha	30 Apr				**19:31-37**
386	Joseph of Arimathaea took Christ's body down Golgotha	30 Apr	27:57-58	**15:42-45**	23:50-52	19:38
387	Jesus' body was prepared for burial Jerusalem	30 Apr	27:59	15:46	23:53	19:38-40
388	Jesus' body was buried in the sepulchre Jerusalem	30 Apr	27:60	15:46	23:53	19:41-42
389	Mary Magdelene and Mary watched the burial Jerusalem	30 Apr	27:61	15:47	23:55-56	
390	The tomb was sealed and a guard placed Jerusalem	30 Apr	**27:62-66**			

Period 11—Christ's Resurrection and Ascension
(Sunday, April 9, 30 A.D. to Thursday, May 18, 30 A.D.)

Event No.	Event	Yr. & Mo.	Matthew	Mark	Luke	John
391	A great earthquake; the tomb opened by an angel Jerusalem	30 Apr	**28:2-4**			
392	Many graves were opened and dead saints arose Jerusalem	30 Apr	**27:52-53**			
393	Three Marys and others came to the tomb Jerusalem	30 Apr	28:1	**16:1-4**	24:1-3, 10	20:1
394	Women told by an angel that Christ was risen Jerusalem	30 Apr	**28:5-6**			
395	Two angels inside the tomb sent women to tell Peter Jerusalem	30 Apr	28:7	16:5-7	**24:4-8**	20:11-13
396	Mary Magdelene told Peter and John about the tomb Jerusalem	30 Apr			24:10-12	**20:2-10**
397	Jesus appeared to Mary Magdelene at the tomb Jerusalem	30 Apr		16:9		**20:14-17**
398	Mary Magdelene told the disciples who she saw Jerusalem	30 Apr		**16:10-11**		
399	Jesus appeared to the women Jerusalem	30 Apr	**28:9-10**			
400	Chief priests bribed the guards to lie Jerusalem	30 Apr	**28:11-15**			